The 10 Principles of Open Business

Building success in today's open economy

The 10 Principles of Open Business

By

David Cushman

with

Jamie Burke

palgrave
macmillan

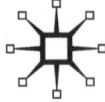
First published 2014 by
PALGRAVE MACMILLAN

Palgrave Macmillan in the UK is an imprint of Macmillan Publishers Limited, registered in England, company number 785998, of Houndmills, Basingstoke, Hampshire RG21 6XS.

Palgrave Macmillan in the US is a division of St Martin's Press LLC, 175 Fifth Avenue, New York, NY 10010.

Palgrave Macmillan is the global academic imprint of the above companies and has companies and representatives throughout the world.

Palgrave® and Macmillan® are registered trademarks in the United States, the United Kingdom, Europe and other countries.

ISBN 978-1-349-46723-5   ISBN 978-1-137-34704-6 (eBook)

DOI 10.1057/9781137347046

This book is printed on paper suitable for recycling and made from fully managed and sustained forest sources. Logging, pulping and manufacturing processes are expected to conform to the environmental regulations of the country of origin.

A catalogue record for this book is available from the British Library.

A catalog record for this book is available from the Library of Congress.

Typeset by MPS Limited, Chennai, India.

For Suzanne and Freya

Contents

List of Figures and Tables

Figure

Table

Foreword

Right time, right book. There is no doubt that the world is in transition. Technology, customers, and economics are driving that change. At the center of that change is the demand from customers, for transparency, trust, and collaboration. The connected nature of these technologies, and the shift in power to customers is creating new businesses and new business models.

These demands will not cease, and why should they? The question is how businesses react to these changes, resist or embrace, control or collaborate. I would argue that there has never been a more important time for businesses to open up and partner with all. By 'all' I mean, businesses will find new partnerships with other businesses, create new services in collaboration with customers, and share their assets in a way that creates new innovation.

Open networks are more collaborative, more creative, and more generative. David's book sets out an important action plan, a set of components that any business should consider if it is to make the most of what is a very exciting revolution in business. Perhaps by embracing the principles of Open Business, we can all create a more sustainable model for growth, something the world really needs.

It's clear that this disruption will lead to new models for business growth. That's exciting, but also challenges much of what defined business in the last decade. This book is an exciting rallying cry for the future business; one that is a productive collaboration between customers and the businesses which seek to earn their loyalty. Many of us are on that road to the future already. I would urge you to read and act.

Matt Atkinson
Chief Marketing Officer
Tesco PLC

Acknowledgments

With sincere thanks to: Sarah Du Heame and Jeremy Hicks, Steffen Hück, Jason Fashade, Ilkut Terzioglu, Lidia Miras Martinez, Kevin Hanney, Marc God, Franz Patzig, Stephan Junghanns, Dinis Guarda, Gianluigi Cuccureddu, Francesco Cuccureddu, Ruben Miras Martinez, Elise Vermersch, Andrea Colaianni, Michael Litman, Sophie Warren, Giulio Vaiuso and everyone else who worked with 90:10 Group (for sharing our purpose).

Luis Suarez (the IBM one, not the football one ...), Rebecca Caroe, Euan Semple, Ted Shelton, Mark Adams, Lee Bryant, Tomi Ahonen, Jonathan MacDonald, Chris Thorpe, Sandrine Desbarbieux, Roland Harwood, Ollie Worsfold, Paul Askew, Gregory Lent, Jon Williams, Stephen Waddington, Violetta Ihalainen, Professor Malcolm McDonald, the team at The Social Partners and at Grey London and everyone who joined in the journey as clients, challengers, or supporters – for opening doors.

Finally, thank you to the team at Palgrave Macmillan and in particular to Eleanor Davey-Corrigan, Anna Keville, Briar Towers, Jamie Forrest, and Tamsine O'Riordan for their enthusiasm, belief, and encouragement.

Introduction: Starting from a Different Place

If you were starting out in business today, would you recreate your business along traditional lines?

Knowing what we now know about how new technologies have disrupted traditional business processes (from marketing to customer service, from raising capital to delivering innovation) would you choose to rebuild it as you find it around you?

If you're not quite sure how to answer that, JP Rangaswami – accidental economist, turned accidental technologist – has a straightforward and stark answer for you: "Trying to create an industrial era firm in a network age is plain, blind, stupidity."

Which is all very well. But what to do about it?

The 10 Principles of Open Business laid out in the chapters that follow are intended to be a serious, challenging, wide-ranging but ultimately practical guide to how your organization can reconfigure itself for the 21st century.

This is organizational design which takes account of the world as it actually is, rather than as it once was; that is – the world in which we now find ourselves.

The Principles are founded on hands-on experience built on the facts of today's economy – one which demands ever greater connectedness, openness, and meaning from the relationships organizations have with their stakeholders.

Through the 10 Principles of Open Business we will define how businesses and other institutions must adapt to both survive and thrive. We provide a simple and practical way to assess your own organization and offer hard-won expertise from practitioners to help you take the first steps toward becoming an Open Business, providing case studies and interviews with leading proponents along the way.

Massive change is ripping through our world. You will have noticed. The web changes the business of organization, and the organization of business.

You will have noticed that old media isn't what it was. A Pew survey at the end of 2010 found the number of people getting their news online had surpassed newspapers for the first time. In Britain, Twitter is now read by more people each morning than the total circulation of all of the nation's daily newspapers. YouTube attracts greater viewing figures, and for longer, than anything mainstream broadcast can produce.

You will have noticed massive new companies mushrooming out of virtually nothing, while seemingly immutable giants crumble and fall. Kodak's demise in the same week of April 2012 that Instagram (a photo app for your smartphone) was sold to Facebook for $1bn offers an ironic illustration.

You will have noticed that trust in politicians and policemen, in banks and in brands, has tumbled. No organization has any sustainable future without trust.

The 10 Principles acknowledge the epoch-making shift happening around us and deliver a way in which its impact needs no longer be dealt with on an issue-by-issue basis. Reactive piecemeal tactics in too many organizations have created a permanent state of panic-ridden catch-up for many, in which learnings are lost in silos and failures swept under carpets.

The 10 Principles of Open Business offer an holistic strategic solution, leap-frogging the tick-box exercise of simple implementation of social technologies. They make organizations future-ready like never before.

Why is this important and why now?

Many of the greatest success stories of the 21st century are built on multiple Open Business principles: Google, Apple, and Amazon among the more famous. Many of its biggest failures aren't and won't be.

According to IBM's CEO survey in May 2012, companies that outperform their sector are 30% more likely to identify "Openness" as a key factor in their success, with particular benefits for collaboration and innovation. Companies are 50% more likely to outperform their rivals and grow sustainable profit following this approach, according to McKinsey.

Businesses unwilling to respond face increasing disruption and competition

Businesses starting today build on the 10 Principles from the word go. They do so because the principles are self-evident to those growing up in our networked world. They know they are simply the most effective way of taking greatest advantage of the world as it exists today. This places them at significant competitive advantage over those who are not seeking to apply the principles for legacy or other reasons.

If Open is the new normal – as UK Deputy Prime Minister Nick Clegg stated at the 2013 G8 summit in London – then so is disruption.

Theory from practice

Your author and his Open Business partner learnt from doing.

Long, hard experience in media, advertising, PR, social media, and business led us to a shared belief in Open Business as the natural next step in, and best fit with, an ever more connected and collaborative world.

We understood that there was much more than Facebook Likes and Twitter Followers to be acquired from the fact that we had all become publishers, marketers, participants (and would-be partners) in making the things that matter most to us.

That is what led us to founding 90:10 Group – a consultancy built to inspire Open Business. In a little over three years we grew to more than 50 employees in eight countries with revenues of £3.5m. We did it, developing the market, the products, and the skills as we went, in the toughest economic climate since World War II.

In those three short years, with a diverse array of often brave and wise clients, including Honda Europe, First Capital Connect, Bupa, Carlson Wagonlit, Citrix, Tesco, MasterCard Europe, Visit Britain, The *Guardian*, Microsoft Advertising, City & Guilds, France Televisions, AgeUK, and more, we pushed boundaries, challenged orthodoxies, and continuously reinvented approaches.

And at the end of the journey we arrived at the 10 Principles.

In the spirit of Open Business they are now yours to use. We urge you to create value for all with them.

Don't wait a single moment ...

Introduction: Defining Open Business – and Its Benefits

An Open Business is one which uses its available resources to discover people who care about the same Purpose it does, brings those people together, and joins with them to achieve that Purpose.

It is designed from the outset to scale through participation. It makes partners of customers.

Open Businesses think of themselves as platforms to deliver a shared purpose – one which inspires and drives those inside the organization while attracting and enabling crowds of supporters outside. In so doing they access a wealth of resource that closed businesses have put up barriers to.

They are Purpose-led, platform-thinking organizations.

By bringing together people to surface their concerns, and working with them to support them in resolving the things that matter to them, they are able to create products and services which are a better fit with the real needs of those for whom they are intended.

You may have heard the term "social business" referenced. Many technology vendors point to it as the application of social technologies within the organization. Some think a little more grandly about it, as genuinely transformative.

There's little wrong with social business and much that is good. But we find it rarely inspires business leaders. Few CEOs will feel comfortable with the thought of turning their business into a social one. The term creates unhelpful left-leaning mental blocks.

But which CEO doesn't want to put the customer at the heart of what they do and drive more innovation?

Opening up to customers and stakeholders and their networks of peers, and their thoughts, and their creative energy, and their passion, and their time, offers an opportunity for something more sensibly owned by the senior team than the IT department.

So what are the differences between Social and Open Business?

Here are three, each of which is critical in transforming the way you do business: tools vs behaviors; messages vs products; customers vs partners.

1 Social is about the tools – Open about behaviors:

Often social business conversations focus on implementing software. Open Business urges you to think behaviors first. What are people doing, what can and will they do? If you are starting with tools you are likely starting in the wrong place.

2 Social is more about messages – Open is more about production:

Open Business urges you to consider ways of making things with the people for whom they are intended; for the best possible fit with real need; for efficiency; for results people care about. Messages are an outcome of this process – not its purpose. Talk "social" and all roads will lead you back to messages.

3 Social is customer-centric – Open makes partners of customers:

Stop thinking about customers. Customers are people you intend to do things to. Open Business urges you to think about the long-suffering customer as a partner to work with, instead. It pushes those people deep into the production process – right to the start, to join with and be supported by the organization in delivering the things all parties want – all partners want.

To become an Open Business is not as easy as starting as one.

The new competitors for established business – and those who are yet to emerge – will find it easier to scale, react to, and meet customer need as a result of launching with the 10 Principles as their start point.

But by following the 10 Principles leaders of established businesses have the opportunity to reconfigure their organizations to take on their new competitors, with the same advantages as the new would seek to turn against the old.

The 10 Principles considered in depth in the following chapters are:

1 Purpose:

Purpose is the why, it is the belief which all your stakeholders share and to which all your organization's actions are aligned. Your products/services are proof of that shared purpose.

2 Open Capital:

Using crowd-funding platforms or principles to raise capital through micro-investments.

3 Networked organization:

The organization functions as a platform connecting internal networks to the external for a common purpose.

4 Shareability:

Packaging knowledge for easy and open internal and external sharing.

5 Connectedness

Connecting all employees to one another and externally through open social media.

6 Open Innovation:

Innovating with partners, and sharing risk and reward in the development of products, services, and marketing.

7 Open Data:

Making your data freely available to those outside your organization who can make best use of it.

8 Transparency:

Decisions, and the criteria on which they are based, are shared openly.

9 Member/Partner-led:

Your organization is structured around the formal co-operation of employees, customers, and partners for their mutual social, economic, and cultural benefit.

10 Trust:

Mutually assured reliance on the character, ability, strength, or truth of the partnership.

In each chapter we define and describe one principle and set a "goal state" and "worst case" scenario. We also provide practical first steps you can take to move your organization toward the goal state for that principle.

Taken together you will be on firm foundations for becoming an Open Business with all the benefits that delivers, including:
- A greater sense of doing business that benefits the society in which you operate
- More attraction and retention of the right talent *and* customers
- Better market and customer knowledge
- Better fit with customer need
- Accelerated and more successful innovation
- Evidence-based decision-making
- New access to capital
- More effective knowledge management

- Improved internal and external collaboration and idea generation
- Lower (distributed) risk through networks of partners
- A greater sense of customer and employee "ownership" through the democratization of business
- Raised levels of trust – and the customer and employee loyalty and satisfaction which derives from this.

Introduction: Tesco PLC – an Open Business

"… the objective was to rebuild this business to be a partner, not a predator."

Matt Atkinson, CMO, Tesco PLC

If you think for one minute that Open Business is a bit "out there" for you, perhaps too soft-centered to be good business, let me introduce you to Tesco PLC – an Open Business.

Tesco PLC is a legendary British business. Founded as a group of market stalls by Jack Cohen in 1919 it went from a down-market also-ran grocer of the 1970s to become the dominant force in UK retailing and the second largest retailer in the world (measured by profit).

Today it can sell you pretty much everything you need from food to clothes, to home furnishings, to financial services. It owns a restaurant chain. It has dabbled in cars. It will even buy your "unwanted" gold.

Its greatest period of growth came with the 1990s and Tesco's decision to diversify in both products and geography. Critical in this was a reposition – shifting from its perception as a pile-it-high-and-sell-it-cheap retailer to one which would appeal across all social groups. It re-invented the concept of good/better/best with its Value/Own Label/Finest ranges.

In the mid-1990s it had just 500 stores. Fifteen years later it had 2500.

But just because you are successful does not mean your customers love you. In fact, in the case of Tesco, their customers did not like them at all.

That shook Tesco. Eventually. But it was a truth that took time to sink in. While the profits kept rolling in it was hard to imagine they might be doing something wrong.

But in the real world everyone knew stories about how hard Tesco was on its suppliers, or heard the negative impact giant Tesco stores had on traditional market town communities.

The Tescopoly Alliance launched in 2006 to "highlight and challenge the negative impacts of Tesco's behaviour along its supply chains both in the UK and internationally, on small businesses, on communities and the environment." Its members included Friends of the Earth and War on Want.

Tescopoly's "Every Little Hurts" tag-line painfully subverted Tesco's own ad slogan "Every Little Helps." Even though the organization's stated aim was to secure local and national legislation to curb the power of all the major British supermarkets, Tesco paid the price for being biggest by becoming the supermarket most associated with and targeted by the campaign.

In October 2012 Tesco posted its first decline in profits in two decades.

Matt Atkinson joined as group marketing and chief digital officer in late 2011.

He joined a business where recently appointed CEO Phillip Clarke was already embracing Open principles. As Matt puts it there was already: "A great platform on which to build."

When I visited him at his offices early in 2012 he was already being clear about the road ahead. Tesco, he said, wanted to be an Open Business.

By January 2013 he had been made CMO – replacing 30-year Tesco veteran Tim Mason (who had also held the title of deputy CEO).

What surprised Matt was how much of an open door he found himself pushing – how much of "Open" was already there, latent in the DNA of the business.

The threat to its future posed by the hardening of its customers, and the broader public, against it had proved exactly the trigger the senior team needed to re-activate that DNA and build on it for the open future.

Open Business isn't something you can layer on. Not if you want it to work.

"We see this as a cultural imperative.

"The first place you have to get to is that Open is a good thing," says Matt.

"You have to get the company to realize that there are some choices to be made in the world today. And the choices are: be closed – try and build value in a closed system and manage and try to control of everything. Or be Open and realize there are lots of benefits from being open, realize there are some risks but that the benefits far outweigh the risks.

"That journey, from being closed to open is a sort of philosophical journey into which the culture of the organization has to lean in and commit."

So how has an idea like Open Business managed to become the guiding principle In a behemoth of a profit-driven corporation, like Tesco?

"To be honest with you, there was no grand one-off presentation. It has been a conversation," says Matt.

And there were some external provocations which helped to make the case.

First, Tesco gathered insight. It commissioned future-facing work around the globe and took a long hard look at the world we see today – and looked from here, into the distant future.

"We realized that our future was much more about being connected and open and about using our skill and our scale to make a difference to that open world."

Second, Tesco commissioned the Reputation Institute – headquartered in New York and Copenhagen. They worked with the senior team to assess the reputation of the organization with its stakeholders. The fundamental output of that was to tell Tesco it had a trust issue.

The Institute's argument was that for Tesco to get the performance it deserves it had to get people to understand why Tesco does what it does – and why that meant it should be trusted.

The third factor was having the right leadership.

"And we were lucky enough to have a CEO (Philip Clarke – the man charged with picking up where Sir Terry Leahy left off in 2011) who believes in the Open world," says Matt.

The fourth is that you are the kind of organization which already has Open in its blood.

"It's funny to say it, but if you think about Tesco, our advantage is an inherent belief that we are for everybody and that we are a democratic brand," said Matt.

"It's our belief that everyone deserves good food, quality food. We should provide it in an accessible way to the highest possible standard and welcome everybody in," he added.

"I haven't had to give the business a personality transplant – and I don't think that's possible. A lot of the beliefs were already here. Some were sleeping and needed resurrecting, some needed a refresh."

It was by digging into its core beliefs that Tesco rediscovered its reason to be. Or as this book would describe it, its Principle 1 of the 10: Purpose – the "Why" of the organization.

"That was an interesting thing. We didn't quite know that's why we exist. We are the biggest broad church in Britain and we'd almost forgotten that," explained Matt.

Rediscovering this truth has been a core part of the journey. It explains why Tesco came up with the "good-better-best" concept, for example.

"We wanted a solution that served every customer so that you could configure your shopping basket to your needs and we used our scale to deliver against all of those needs reasonably well."

Others may copy – Matt argues – but with Tesco there is an inherent belief that it is an Open Business which welcomes everybody which drives it to create innovations of that kind.

Will that culture take Tesco to the next step of the journey – to co-create with its customers the products, the services, the business itself?

"We do a lot of collaborative insights work through a thing called Tesco's Families.

"We're developing a sort of advocacy platform where we can have much more open conversation with customers about our products and services and what we do and we are planning to do more in that space," says Matt.

Again, there have been external triggers which have accelerated the drive to Open. In 2013 a powerful one came in what Matt refers to as "Horse-gate." Throughout the early months of 2013 British consumers were rocked time and again by discoveries of the use of the wrong meat in the products they thought they could trust. Four Tesco ready meals (from a range of 1000s) were found to contain small percentages of horse meat instead of the beef the packaging described.

It was another undermining of trust in brands. What was interesting to many observers was how various brands responded.

Findus famously passed the buck – blaming its supplier. That failed the basic test: Customers bought your product because it had your brand on it, not your supplier's – you are responsible.

Others skulked around assuming the best or hoping they too wouldn't get caught out. Few large retailers or low-cost caterers came through completely clean.

Across Europe IKEA's famous canteen meatballs were taken off the menu and Nestle withdrew products in Spain, Italy, and France. In the UK tests found horse meat in products at Makro, Taco Bell, Compass, Whitbread's pub restaurants (such as those typically located with Premier Inns), Morrisons, Aldi, Iceland, Lidl, Co-op, and Asda.

Sainsbury made precautionary withdrawals and Waitrose took its frozen meatballs off the shelves when they found traces of pork in them.

Yes, Tesco was tainted too. But of all those having to face the music it was Tesco which was first and loudest in response. And not just with words.

"Horse-gate was a tipping point for us. In the old world we would never have reacted in the way that we did. We were first out of the blocks, we accepted responsibility and said we were going to do something about it.

"That was a sign of what has happened here. We didn't even discuss the risks, nobody said 'is that legal or not legal,' or that we shouldn't do this, or that. It seemed like it was the right and natural thing to do," said Matt.

CEO Philip Clarke took to YouTube to tell customers how important their trust in his company was and to explain what he was doing in response.

In a three-minute piece to camera he uses the word "trust" nine times. That is an average of once every 20 seconds.

The rapid response included a commitment to conduct a root and branch review of the supply chain and production processes with the ambition to deliver the best supply chain in the world.

To live out the promise of traceability and accountability, Tesco also committed to launching an open website giving every one of its customers oversight of not only the finished process, but also a way of holding the company to account for its progress toward this new goal. And to back up the promise, if there was ever cause for concern about a Tesco product it would be replaced at no extra charge.

The reason Tesco was able to respond so rapidly and so positively was that this way of thinking had already become natural. There had been no need to create a new manifesto – no need to describe a new default position.

"It's just become part of the narrative in the business. It's part of the new core purpose (launched at the end of 2012) and the conversations leading to that had included opening up a new set of leadership skills," said Matt – and Horse-gate provided the first opportunity for these to be tested.

"The objective wasn't 'To Become An Open Business,' no, the objective was to rebuild this business so it's a partner not a predator," said Matt.

Open Business provided the framework to reach that goal.

"We want to be wanted and needed in the world," said Matt.

A similar vision sits at the heart of automotive manufacturer Honda's core beliefs. Its ambition is to be "a company that society wants to exist."

Companies which don't take this view cannot expect to take advantage of the skills, efforts, and ideas which could otherwise be available to them from the communities in which they operate. Which of us wants to partner to help companies which do not act as if they operate in the same resource-constrained world as the rest of us?

Matt continues: "We should be using our scale for good for the benefit and welfare of the communities we serve. We should do great things for customers that matter in their lives.

"As a result of that, we'll be trusted."

The thinking has taken Tesco to a world-changing and fantastically positive customer-and-staff rallying position. It had to be in the DNA to bring out, there had to be a clear sense of a future goal and there had to be a leader that believed. But what was also required was a crisis.

"Our burning platform was coming to the point of having to ask ourselves how did we become so not loved, so not wanted? Why is it that people are saying they don't like us and that we don't do good things? Why is it that people are saying we put profit ahead of their interest? Why was all this happening when, fundamentally, if you cut a Tesco person in half that was absolutely not what they were about."

Matt believes it was a natural and inevitable conclusion to all their thinking and to their crises, to become more open.

"You can't become a more wanted part of people's lives in a closed way – at least we don't believe that you can," he added.

The "Tesco in Society 2013 Report" outlines what Tesco is now aiming to achieve.

It is enshrined in the new core purpose: "We Make What Matters Better, Together."

The Tesco website now states:

> The World has changed and we have to change to reflect this. It used to be the case that more was better but now it's about making what matters better … We want to make a positive and lasting difference for our customers, colleagues and the communities we serve … Our Values guide us to change for the better and to change in better ways …. Our Values are:
>
> • No one tries harder for customers
> • We treat everyone how we like to be treated
> • We use our scale for good
>
> These aren't gimmicks, they aren't just words, they're fundamental to how we do business.

Purpose-driven. Open. The world's second biggest retailer is becoming an Open Business not for PR, not for appearances, not to meet the aspirations of some hippy-tinged idyll, but because it is the right business decision for the 21st century.

And it is not alone, as other examples throughout this book will illustrate.

"I think it's a massive trend. In retail that means more convenient shopping, more local. What are the categories that are in decline? Frozen and ready meals."

The fact that people want more of their food to be local and fresh is part of the return of a sense of community which the web has played its part in. The web reveals our connectedness and feeling connected means feeling a part of something over which you can and should have influence.

"What made us brilliantly successful in the past has been our customer innovation and the operationalization of that innovation into supply chains, formats and consistency of offer.

"In the next 10 years it is very clear that what will make us successful is more intelligence, de-averaging the formats, blending our multi-channel offering and having more personality to help us be both more helpful and relevant to our customer," said Matt.

What that means is that the store manager of the future should know their loyal customer base and be working alongside them in the community.

"I'd want him (or her) to be known and valued in their local community," said Matt.

For those who remember life when supermarkets began in the UK, that was pretty much how things were. Indeed right into the 1980s local managers had their own relationships with suppliers, their own teams of buyers, their own roots in the communities they served.

Is there enough value in closer relationships with customers, that matter more to customers, versus the massive scale efficiencies of centralized buying and stock control?

Tesco is betting the farm on the belief that there certainly is better business in meeting the needs of their diverse customers more accurately through responsiveness and relevance.

"I think digital and social media allow you to operationalize that on a scale basis," he adds.

"I remember making a presentation 15 years ago when I talked about what I believed the future of marketing to be about and I talked about this sort of marketing automation which is becoming a reality today," says Matt.

Tesco already has an outstanding ability to gather and use data about its customers, whether that is direct purchase behavior via its Clubcard loyalty and reward scheme or through how customers talk about it and its products through its activity in social media (its main Facebook page has more than 1.2m Likes, for example) and its monitoring of conversations in open social media.

But there is more and more effective use of this to come which could bring back the local relevance and community value of stores as they once existed.

"What we really have is an engine to help the customer in a much more effective way. They don't see the engine but we can use it to anticipate and respond helpfully. We are just on the cusp of being able to do this in the sort of way that delivers what a local store manager embedded in their own communities pre-1980s knew from their daily one-to-one interactions with customers and their ability to 'take the temperature' for needs specific to their store and being able to solve them at the time and the place the solution is needed," said Matt.

"If your core purpose is about what matters to customers and how you can make those things better by what you do, If that's the quest then you ask yourself how do I use technology and systems and processes to enable me to do that?" said Matt.

Today's technology, data and open communications, combined with Tesco's scale means it's so much more efficient to do that today.

If part of being an Open Business is the belief that you act as a platform to bring together those who share your aims to work together to achieve them, then what are those ambitions for the platform that Tesco is working toward becoming?

Matt believes there are two parts to that. The first is from the platform to the individual, and the second from the platform to the individual and their community.

The first part, he said, was driven by the idea that "No one tries harder for customers."

"The only problem was we weren't quite living it," Matt admits.

"We've refocused our effort on that to be clear about how we want to do that and who we want to do that for. It's really all about us demonstrating our loyalty to customers – and if customers feel that, then they will give us their loyalty.

"The other bit is the introduction of a new value which is 'using our scale for good,' so that we are a welcome member of the communities we serve."

This do-good message centers on future-gazing which has identified a series of problems which Tesco can use its scale to help to solve.

But this "doing good" is more than just a program of corporate social responsibility. It makes doing good, good business. By solving each of the concerns it has identified Tesco will play a positive role in helping to sustain communities of customers with cash in their pockets.

"It doesn't take you long to get to three things which we feel are very, very important – that matter and which I think any customer would thank us for doing," says Matt.

The first is providing opportunities for young people in their communities.

"We really want to do something about that. It's a big problem," he says.

The second is finding a way to inspire people to have a happy, healthy life.

"We've really got an opportunity to help people change the way they eat and live."

The third area is waste.

"This one we see as particularly mad, based on looking into the future of population growth and climate challenges. It is extraordinary that we live in a world where one part of the world is eating itself to death and the other half is starving."

Matt believes Tesco can help create communities in which young people have plenty of interesting opportunities, in which people are happy and healthy and which isn't wasteful and is productive.

"That, to me, sounds like a pretty good place to be. It's our belief that a happy healthy community with good opportunities for young people is a good place to be doing business," he says.

These are clear goals which others can believe in and which others could be gathered toward to help achieve. That is a critical element of any Open Business.

Attaining the kind of buy-in, the sense of partnership that a shared purpose can achieve should lead to a next step in the development of an Open Business. Right now Tesco's technologies and processes are relatively passive recipients of the understanding of customer needs.

Is it ready to move toward a proactive relationship, in which customers help to make the decisions in the business and start to feel a sense of ownership – of leadership?

"Absolutely. We are creating platforms to collaborate. You have to declare your interest and then enable people to join in with you on those quests. We're not quite there yet because we haven't yet fully declared those interests."

But by the time this book publishes in 2014, that's likely to be underway. Tesco will be declaring its Purpose(s), and indicating its willingness to commit capital, resources, and know-how in support of them.

If, for example, your goals and ambitions coincide with Tesco's dreams for young people, then Matt hopes Tesco can act as a platform for action you would choose to contribute to.

"We think people will. In today's world you can set up a web page and state what you are interested in and soon enough people find you and join in," said Matt.

"We want to achieve these goals in an open way. All we are doing is bringing capital, resource, some knowledge."

Matt sums up the difference from old to new way (from closed to open) as, "Historically we'd have got in a room and said 'how can we do this on our own?' Now what we are saying is how can we do this with others?"

How will Tesco measure success? We're entering a new world which is perhaps a very different shape and which requires new dimensions to measure. But there are some essentials.

"We're doing a bit of work which basically comes down to how much we are trusted. Brand equity drives performance, low brand equity is a drag on performance," he says.

From understanding what are the drivers of brand equity for your brand you soon get a steer on what to measure. Trust is a critical part for most.

"You can't build trust in a closed way," Matt reiterates. "We empirically know that an open system creates value for that. That's the plan, that's the purpose, that's the strategy. Are we relentlessly obsessing about its bottom line effect? No.

"But I think we are trying to work out, for example, how much money we should put into 'using our scale for good.'

"It's not that we don't want to put the money in, but we are a business. We've made the decision as part of our investment strategy and our business plan that we invest – just as in computers or concrete – in 'scale for good' because it is part of how the sales get generated. And it's the right thing to do," says Matt.

Not only does it make business sense, it's also hugely motivational. It's the "why" people come to work.

Tesco is part way through a potentially massive transformation to take a new role in the lives of its customers and of their communities. That's not easy to pull off.

What are the essentials in making it happen?

Matt says: "Get your core purpose nailed. Apart from that you have to have a burning platform around which that core purpose gets ignited and I think you've got to have a really good narrative that everyone understands. It must not be a peripheral activity, this new way of doing core purpose.

"It also has to be a virtuous circle which has to be about what the business does, not what corporate affairs communicates. It has to be an inherent part of the brand."

Open Business is a framework for the future – in use today.

Purpose

Definition

Purpose is the why. It is the belief which all your stakeholders share and to which all your organization's actions are aligned. Your products/services are proof of that shared purpose.

As you might expect from our definition of Open Business ("one which uses its available resources to discover people who care about the same Purpose it does, brings those people together and joins with them to achieve that Purpose"), Purpose is mission critical.

Most organizations are good at "What" they do and "How" they do it. But ask them "Why?" and things get trickier. How does yours score? See our Goal State/Worst Case at the end of the chapter.

Most, when asked about Purpose, will point to Mission Statements. Unfortunately in the majority of cases a Mission Statement begs a further question: Why?

Many are written along the lines of intended outputs, "To be No. 1 in our chosen markets and sectors returning maximum value to shareholders." Or, "To be the most admired."

Why?

That "Why?" is important. It is what brings people together, motivates them, and inspires them to support your cause. In our connected world, in which an organization's role is to act as a platform to help others achieve a collective shared Purpose, it is essential. It is how you succeed.

It can't be just any old "thing." It has to be something that matters. Something about the world you want to put right. Something that matters to you and to others. Something to believe in.

Who will give you their time to help you shape your products, services, or business if they don't believe in the same things you do? There are plenty of other brands out there they can be giving their attention, knowledge, skills, time, and money.

As Mark Earls (and we'll hear more from Mark shortly) puts it in his book *Herd* (Wiley 2007): "Find Your Purpose Idea and Live it."

It should be what gets you out of bed in the morning, it should be what inspires staff and partners to join you, it should be what attracts people to support you on your journey because it is their journey, too.

Get it right, truly believe in it, and express that belief through everything you do and you'll find, as artist and marketer Hugh MacLeod draws it: "The market for something to believe in is infinite."

express that belief through everything you do

Businesses which live and breathe their Purpose need to spend less resource on telling people what they believe. Customers can see it for themselves, not through what the company says, but by what it does.

Google is a great example. Now with $94bn in assets and annual revenues of over $50bn (2012 figures), it lives the same Purpose as it did when it was founded in 1998: "To organize the world's information and make it universally useful."

That informs what they do and what they don't do, their approach to data and openness (universally useful), it guides their acquisition strategy (is it going to help us achieve our Purpose?), and it acts as a motivator to those who may want to support Google or work for it.

That Purpose is supported by a set of principles which act as guidance on how Googlers (as staff are known) should behave in seeking to achieve that Purpose. These have proved essential as the business scales – and does so in a distributed rather than hierarchical model. They frame the Google culture.

These principles famously include Don't Be Evil (more accurately You Can Make Money Without Doing Evil). Others are You Don't Have to Wear A Suit to Be Serious, Focus On The User And All Else Will Follow, It's Best To Do One Thing, Really, Really Well, and Democracy On The Web Works.

In line with their belief in the principles of Open, Google publishes all 10 of its own principles on its corporate website – and calls on the world to hold them to account.

Ask any Googler. They'll know all about their Purpose.

Compare that to Yahoo. Once Google's greatest global rival, now a pale, distant shadow of a competitor.

According to an article by Adam Lashinsky in *Fortune* published in February 2007, Yahoo's Terry Semel was interviewed about Purpose in summer 2006. He had been CEO for five years at that time.

> After an uncomfortably long pause, Semel replied: "I don't know that we have a motto. Well, the mission of the company is; Deliver great value to our consumers and, basically, value them."

Actually, at the time, Yahoo did have a mission at least. It was (the clearly little known):

> To be the most essential global Internet service for consumers and businesses.

No wonder it was little known. You have to Do in line with your Purpose – not just write it down. And even by 2006 it was clear Yahoo was far from essential for either consumers or businesses. If anyone could claim that position it was their great rival Google.

Yahoo – which was incorporated in 1995 – had been overtaken by a faster growing, Purpose-led business.

Yahoo wasn't founded to be the most essential Internet service for consumers and businesses but for something far simpler – and closer in spirit to Google's own Purpose: "A way to keep track of personal interests on the Internet."

There is a kernel of that in the "Mission" Yahoo rolled out in 2007: "To connect people to their passions, their communities, and the world's knowledge."

Yahoo's difference was in connecting people to their interests. It was a people-focused philosophy. If they had been living it then perhaps when Facebook and Twitter first emerged Yahoo would have been first in the queue of suitors.

While Google's Purpose has remained rock solid, Yahoo's has been fluid. The latest on its corporate website in 2013 stated: "Yahoo! is focused on making the world's daily habits inspiring and entertaining."

What does that mean they should and shouldn't do today?

Purpose is hugely important – way more than most senior teams realize (witness Mr Semel). If you don't know where you are going, how are you going to get there?

In 2012, Yahoo's revenues were less than 10% of Google's, their assets around 15%.

That's 10 times the revenue. That's how important Purpose is.

* * *

Mark Earls has worked with some of the world's biggest brands and organizations, helping them find and deliver change and value through

Purpose. He is a former executive planning director EMEA and chair of the Global Planning Council at Ogilvy & Mather (London and Frankfurt) and author of not only *Herd* (previously referenced) but also (with Professors Alex Bentley and Mike O'Brien) *I'll Have What She's Having – Mapping Social Behavior* (MIT Press 2011).

Toward the end of the last century Mark Earls was "with a bunch of other crazies" running an independent London-based creative agency called St Luke's. It was there that his thinking around Purpose first emerged.

"I was thinking very hard about the businesses that we all admired. They didn't seem to fit into the cookie-cutter, mechanistic model of business school education or marketing 'how-to's'. They were somehow more interesting."

At the time it was companies like IKEA and Virgin that attracted his attention.

"It struck me that what differentiated these organizations was they believed something," says Mark. IKEA for example has a series of principles its founder set out, best summarized in the IKEA vision which is "To create a better everyday life for the many people."

Note the distinct lack of reference to either furnishings or shareholders in that line.

Most organizations don't believe in something. Instead, as Mark notes, they "nod" to the corporate value statement, they nod to the mission/vision/purpose, they nod to the importance of the brand, and of caring for their customers.

According to Mark, you can spot the organizations for which this is true, because they are the ones that illustrate their nodding in a very corporate, glossy way, through slick video – or through missions articulated without emotion.

"They do it in with no real feeling for the people involved," Mark says.

Many logistics businesses let themselves down in this way, he continues, having worked with many. They talk about how much easier life would be without customers. Passengers get in the way. They spoil and confuse.

"What becomes really clear is how annoying the customer is to them."

The old British Railways, Mark says, would claim it could run a brilliant rail network "if it wasn't for those bloody customers."

"Most boardrooms in the 1990s – and for the early part of this century – really seemed to dislike customers and didn't want to get anywhere near them. Most would rather not be exposed to the messiness of people's lives."

One Twitter account set up by a frustrated rail employee in the UK says it all. It was called @PaxHater (Pax being industry shorthand for passengers).

Real customers and their actual behaviors are difficult to fit on spreadsheets, Mark contends. The culture of business is often about mechanical processes – a poor fit with the more organic reality of their customers' lives.

"In *Herd* … I talk about how management science is rooted in the late 19th-century obsession with machinery, and the view of humans as like machines but lazier and less precise, and less efficient, and less reliable … just less machine-like."

Even now, the idea of really listening to your customers remains a rarity, Mark continues:

"Instead we set up fancy things which are machine-like, systems for listening rather than actually listening. That's why the market research industry is such a huge phenomenon. It's an excuse to intermediate between a business and its customers," says Mark.
"It makes what customers say easy to package, and safe – with none of the anger."

Customers are often grumpy. Corporate HQ would rather not know.

The organizations that we "like" says Mark, or which cause a stir in the culture, are those which are more humane. They make sense in a way which isn't only about pounds and dollars.

The second indicator of businesses lacking this higher purpose, and through this a connection to their humanity, were the KPIs, Mark recalls.

"There was a moment when – so the story goes – the magic circle of Fortune 500 CEOs got together in the very early 90s and said: 'This balancing of shareholder, and stakeholder, and employee, and social … all those interests … it's really hard! So … let's not do it anymore. We're just going to focus on shareholders'."

Whether the moment actually happened or not, the reality was that managers and employees became tools of the shareholder – driven to more and more short-term thinking to deliver next quarter results.

Against this backdrop, the Purpose-driven businesses began to stand out.

Jim Collins and Jerry Porras in their book *Built To Last* (HarperBusiness 1994) drew on a six-year Stanford University Business School study of 18 truly exceptional and long-lasting companies against their like-for-like competitors.

"Their basic observation is that businesses that organize themselves around a purpose, some higher calling, something other than the financial performance of the business, outperform businesses which organize around financial performance. They say it's a 7:1 ratio."

They happen to deliver above-average shareholder return over the medium- and long-term as a consequence.

Purpose can't stop at the boardroom door. The experience the customer has is their contact point.

And the thing that delivers that experience, Marks says, is behavior.

"This connects with a really big agenda that has emerged in the last five or six years," says Mark.

He believes it is now quite clear from the work of Paul Feldwick and Robert Heath (50 Years Using the Wrong Model of TV Advertising, *IJMR*, 50(1), 2008), from the work of Les Binet and Peter Field for the IPA (various), and that of John Kearon and Orlando Wood (at behavior-focused market research business BrainJuicer) that the way television advertising works is not primarily about sending messages.

That would, of course, be our rational expectation. Reach and rational response to the message is where the KPIs are so often focused.

"It's how it makes you feel, not the information it transmits. It's your emotional response not the intellectual (rational) response that is the key thing," says Mark.

Classical economics holds that we are information processors calculating utility and economic value in each transaction. Mark dismisses that view with some choice language. In short, he believes, the Milton Friedman description of a human (that our every choice is aimed at maximizing our benefits and minimizing our costs) is a description of a species that has never existed.

"So, communication is not about sending information."

Being Purpose-led, more connected to emotional rather than simple rational value, therefore offers more effective communication at this all-important emotional level.

"When we look at behavior change in a broader sense, beyond advertising and marketing, it's quite clear that telling people the right or healthy thing to do, even giving them all the information in the world, doesn't tend to work," says Mark.

Rather than information, Mark thinks of communication being gestural – or what linguistic anthropologists would call *phatic* – an expression whose only function is to perform a social task.

An everyday example would be the phrase "You're welcome." We don't say it because we want to convey the information that you are (literally welcome). We use it as a social token in response to being thanked.

"In other words it is through behavior that we generate a response from someone. That starts to explain why Purpose and aligning behavior with it are so important in business," says Mark.

It's true as much for the way businesses are led as for what they would wish to communicate. Tell people how to behave and it's unlikely you'll get them to align. Show them through your own behavior and you will have a much greater chance of communicating and making the change you are aiming for.

And at the business level, the way a business behaves – in everything it does and its people do – is the gestural, emotional, "beyond information" way it communicates.

Understanding Purpose is hard. It demands that we throw away cherished notions of rationality. But against the alternative it starts to feel right …

"Our expectation of customers being able to have completely coherent explanations of how they feel about stuff is entirely unhelpful," says Mark.

The same should be true of employees, Mark believes. He cites award-winning UK broadcaster and innovator, Channel 4.

Channel 4 – for those unfamiliar with terrestrial television in the UK – is a publicly owned but advertising-funded broadcaster. It was originally created, in 1982, to break up the hegemony of the BBC and its independent commercial counterpart ITV, with the aim of creating a thriving independent production sector.

More than 30 years on, it still commands a significant share of the UK broadcast and advertising markets as well as being the driving force – through Film4 – behind many fresh voices in the movie business (such as *Trainspotting*, *The Last King of Scotland*, and *Slumdog Millionaire*).

Even so, when David Abraham become CEO in May 2010 he found an organization suffering after half a decade of what Maggie Brown of the

Guardian newspaper described as a management policy of "doom and gloom" and one which took a cap-in-hand stance toward the taxpayers who own the business.

Few who saw Channel 4's extraordinary coverage of the London 2012 Paralympics (under the Cannes-winning banner of "Superhumans"), or who witnessed the advertising sales team's resolve in resisting the boycott by Group M (the biggest TV advertising buying point in the UK) at the end of 2012, could doubt that this is now a revitalized business.

More evidence presents itself in its continued ability to develop and deliver innovative content, products, and services.

The turnaround required great leadership; a simple, potent strategy based on a profound understanding of the competition and the changing landscape; excellent talent and talent practices; bold and brave creative and technology decisions; hard work and pocketful of luck.

But what really helped pull it together was *Purpose*. More specifically, says Mark, what really helped was Purpose clearly articulated and adopted throughout the organization.

Unusually, Channel 4's Purpose is written into law (both the original founding statute and subsequent amendments essentially describe its remit to be innovative, experimental, and distinctive). But human beings don't work well with statute, which is why David Abraham made recovering a shared sense of Channel 4's Purpose a priority. It would prove a key lever for change in other areas.

"Of course, like any incoming leader, I'm sure he had a number of extremely urgent items in his in-tray (financial, people, technology, marketing, and so on) but the most important one was to challenge the business to re-articulate a sense of *what it is for* … and to bake this into the organization and its daily life," says Mark.

"Once you all know who we are and what we are for, everyday decisions and life-changing ones both become easier: both at the top and the bottom of the business.

"In the big stuff, like how a business organizes itself, what kind of people they hire, and which projects and shows they back. And in the everyday stuff, like how people treat each other and what they do for each other."

It is the widespread nature of such organizational self-knowledge – at an intuitive emotional level – that seems to have empowered the Channel 4 organization and given it back its mojo. They arrived at "Mission with Mischief" as their descriptive Purpose – as David Abraham told his audience at the 2012 Edinburgh International Television Festival.

"It's made them appropriately bold – which is I think why they were able to go for the 2012 Paralympics bid with such a clear and enthusiastic proposal which treated these amazing athletes as they are. 'Superhumans' – the creative theme for their coverage – has rapidly become the default concept for Paralympics sport," says Mark.

As well as generating a raft of award-winning content and advertising (landing a Gold Lion at the Cannes Advertising Festival), it also delivered unforeseen (by outsiders, at least) audience figures and a sense of significant momentum for the organization. Purpose helped it win.

Clarity in Purpose is becoming increasingly essential in distributed (vs centralized command and control) organizations – which is rapidly becoming the majority of organizations today.

If every employee is clear about the Purpose of the organization, if they express this in what they do and it is expressed in what they see of the behaviors of the business and of their colleagues, then they will be better able to make decisions which are truly aligned to the Purpose. Each time they do, they make a positive contribution to the phatic message the business is expressing to its customers.

"People aren't dumb terminals to which you can transmit instructions. Nor can you write even the cleverest algorithm to make them do their stuff. You have to encourage them to use their skill and judgment and a sense of what is right as far the business – and their customer – is concerned," says Mark.

One hundred years ago the majority (roughly 80%) of industry was in extraction and processing, the minority (roughly 20%) in people-related activity. Today that ratio is reversed for most developed countries. The decisions your people make are what drives the success of the business. Ensuring those decisions are made toward your shared goal (Purpose) is therefore more critical than ever.

Since we have seen that telling teams is not enough (and even less likely to succeed in distributed structures), ensuring they know the Purpose, through belief and behaviors, becomes even more essential.

What is your first step as a leader to achieving this?

The first challenge is to "feel" in a passionate way, what matters to you, what matters to people out there and what matters to the world, says Mark.

Most important of all, is what matters to *you*.

"Not just what makes sense on a spreadsheet, not just 'I've got some VCs excited in this,' or, 'I've extrapolated a big ker-ching moment for me in the future.' What beyond all this really means something to you. Why is it such a good thing?"

When the focus is on KPIs, passion doesn't get much of a look in.

"We don't have a culture for this in northern Europe in general. MBAs haven't helped. They have suggested that business is a matter of spreadsheets and rationality, when it is, for the large part, not," Mark argues.

We aren't saying that you should not keep score or give up on measurement. We are saying don't use these as a replacement for what matters, the passion and feeling your decisions are based on.

Purpose is not just for the good times. It can make organizations more resilient in the hard times. It offers a way of protecting your price premium. If yours is just a commodity, if there is no difference between your product and the next in the eyes of the customer, then you will get squeezed.

It even protects against not being best. Mark contends that the technically best thing doesn't always win (the spreadsheet view of the world would always suggest that it should). For example Betamax famously outperformed VHS as a videotape format in the 1980s, but it was VHS that became ubiquitous.

Pepsi is a "better" product than Coke in the blind taste tests. But Coke wins in market after market. It wins, Mark argues, because we all know what Coke is, what it represents to us and other people.

"Wherever you look, whichever market you look at, the most successful is not the best. The most successful is the one that has harnessed Purpose – and also social engagement – it's embedded in what we do," Mark says.

Purpose is one of the key ways in which to embed a product or brand in that social space. "The space between people," as Mark puts it, "not the space between their ears."

the idea takes shape in interaction between people

What he is driving at is the notion that the idea takes shape in interaction between people, not from the individuals. It is shaped in the space between us more than by us.

One way to think about this is by considering how influence actually works. There are many products claiming to inform brands and businesses about who their most influential customers are. Most focus in entirely the wrong place – on the individual. They give a score to a person.

But influence – just like an idea – is a social construct. It can't be constrained within an individual. It only has meaning in its interaction between individuals. The score should more properly go to the sum total of the interactions around the idea.

That kind of reductionism is an easy sell to the world of the spreadsheet – likely because it is a great fit with old certainties about influence from the center. It is comforting. But it is wrong – it's a better fit with the world of broadcast than of organic networks we are now living in. And it won't help you communicate your Purpose.

On the assumption that you have your Purpose – you have found your fire, the thing beyond shareholder value you want to achieve, the belief about something to fix, change, put right that others will emotionally connect with and want to help you achieve (it may even be a rediscovery of the founder's ideals) ... what's your next step? How do you even start to convince your closest colleagues?

Mark refers to Dove – a fast moving consumer good. A soap. What is there to believe in about that?

"I've been lucky enough to work with Sylvia Lagnado in the past, who became global brand director on Unilever's Dove. She and the Ogilvy team working with her clocked the fact that this was just another personal brand – and the world really didn't need any more."

There was at least an interesting back story. Dove had originally been invented as a medical cleanser in World War II. And while that is not directly where its Purpose was reborn, its Purpose did at least emerge from the same "caring about people" place that so many products cannot lay claim to.

But that was not enough. And when the history of the brand does not offer enough, or has become no longer relevant, then you have to ask, "What can we do with this brand? What are our objectives? What is it that matters to us? What agenda can we use this to advance?" These are the questions you can and should be asking of your colleagues.

"It has to be true for you. A number of times I've seen clients I've worked with who see that Purpose is a good thing to adopt. They add it on to their brand key or whatever, so in addition to a proposition they have a purpose," says Mark.

But, he warns: "That kind of misses the point. They know that everyone needs one, and they know for reasons we've discussed that it's important. But it ends up feeling tacked on.

"It's important to strip everything back and ask: 'What are you going to use this business for? What really matters to you in this world that you are going to do more or less of?' It's important to feel it."

In the case of Dove they found their purpose in The Campaign for Real Beauty which had as its Purpose: "to create a world where beauty is a source of confidence and not anxiety."

It championed every woman's right to feel beautiful against the body-and-age Nazis. They did more than say it. They went on to support the messages of the 30-second spots with active support for campaigns to fight (for example) anorexia and to build young women's self-esteem in general. They created a movement. Dove stands for something.

If a soap bar can do it …

Paul Polman, CEO at Unilever since 2007, is taking a Purpose message to his shareholders: something much beyond profit.

Mark says: "He's done a tremendous job in showing them that the only way the business is going to build sustainable growth is by making their footprint on the world smaller – in production (in both ecological and human terms) and in the use of their products.

"He's telling them that Unilever is going to have to teach people how to use products as well as developing products to make less impact on the world. It's brave and it sets up some very clear expectations about the activities they will and won't engage in."

Unilever is not alone in identifying this. Or in saying it. The challenge now is to show through its behavior what it believes in.

In our connected, always-under-observation, everyone-publishing world there is nowhere for saying-it-but-not-doing-it to hide. You will get called out.

There have never been greater drivers for businesses to become Purpose led.

Apart from anything else, it will reconnect you with the world, re-tying those strands cut loose when CEOs first decided that shareholders mattered more than anyone or anything else.

"It's a reversal back to the old days," says Mark, "when corporations felt part of the world and felt a responsibility to it.

"It puts, for example, the corporate tax avoidance discussions we've been having in 2013 in the UK (Google, Starbucks, Amazon, and others have all been accused by Parliamentary Select Committees) into an interesting light.

"Eric Schmidt (executive chairman) of Google famously suggested that it's his job to avoid tax – returning maximum value to the shareholders. But that is too short term a view in the world as we are now finding it. Your job is to build value for the shareholders in the long term – but build value for everyone else as well," says Mark.

The human element in all of this becomes increasingly important, the more our businesses and economies are based on the skills, knowledge, and actions of our people (vs the extracting of resource).

"People are messy, and people are brilliant, and people are scary and unpredictable, creative, conservative, radical, shy, open … they are all of those things but hiding under your table and thinking the spreadsheet will keep you from them is no answer," says Mark.

"Purpose helps you, as a leader, push out what matters throughout the organization."

Founder of outdoor clothing brand Patagonia, Yvon Choinard started his business with a strong Purpose. Since 1986 he has been giving a portion of profits to green causes. The company has always been transparent about (for example) the chemicals it uses – and its effort to use as few as possible.

"Patagonia wants to be in business for a good long time, and a healthy planet is necessary for a healthy business. We want to act responsibly, live within our means and leave behind … an Earth whose beauty and biodiversity is protected for those who come after us," states the company website. "[B]usiness can inspire solutions to the environmental crisis … we owe those that work in the textile industry fair labour practices and safe working conditions."

It doesn't just say. It does.

- The Footprint Chronicles offers a supplier map in an effort to be transparent as a motivator to continue to "reduce the adverse social and environmental impact" of the business.
- The Common Threads Partnership pledges to make only useful clothing that lasts a long time (to ensure you do not buy what you do not need), it offers help in repairing Patagonia gear. Provided you pledge to fix what is broken, it says Patagonia will donate its unsold products to charity – and asks that you sell or pass on what you no longer need to someone who does need it. It welcomes worn out Patagonia gear for recycling and asks that you never just throw it away.
- Employees are given opportunities to help in environmental projects. Every element of the company's impact on the environment is constantly examined with the aim of reducing the bad.

These positive environmental benefits could and should be sold as a positive benefit for a sustainable and healthy business as we have seen in the case of Unilever and as supported by Sir Richard Branson's "Doing good is good for business" philosophy – which lays behind his Virgin Unite initiative (a project to use the entrepreneurial energy of Virgin communities around the world as a force for good).

One challenge to the philosophy has been the legal enshrining of the principle of delivering shareholder value first (at least in Public Limited Companies). With PLCs it's possible for disgruntled shareholders to take directors to court if they don't appear to be seeking to maximize shareholder value.

Patagonia has, in theory, never had to make the case that its Purpose will – in the long run – be better at value creation than a simple profit-first approach – because it is privately owned.

Nonetheless, it has now taken the additional step of enshrining its driving principle in law. In January 2012 it announced it would become one of California's first "Benefit Corporations" – a new legal entity which gives directors the legal right to put social and environmental missions ahead of financial concerns.

Benefit Corporations (which had been placed on to 12 US states' statute books by June 2013) suit the ideas of the environmental lobby very well. But what if your Purpose is not wholly about an environmental or social benefit – or a general public benefit, as the law puts it?

California also now offers the Flexible Purpose Corporation in which founders can write-in a "special mission" into the articles of incorporation. Directors must then take that special aim into account in their decision-making – even at the cost of lower returns for shareholders.

If you're ready to start thinking about how Purpose could benefit your organization, Mark Earls has some simple advice: With your Purpose in mind, list out what you are going to carry on doing and what you are going to stop doing.

"I'm a great fan of back-of-the-envelope strategy. What really matters to you only becomes clear when you are able to say what you like and what you don't like about what you are doing," he says.

"Be really clear what you believe in – that you are not a cookie-cutter business, you are one driven by real values."

Without a Purpose your business is just a loose collection of reporting lines and spreadsheets. And it will lose in the long run.

Summary

Purpose is the Why. It drives growth, inspires and attracts staff, customers, and senior teams, shortcuts decision-making, provides focus, and reduces marketing spend.

Where does your business stand from 1 to 5?

Goal state (*scores 5/5*)

You have a clear "Why" of the organization – why it exists (what is it about the world you are trying to put right/fix, etc.) Everyone who knows of you knows of your Purpose. One hundred percent of your actions are aligned with and express that Purpose.

Worst case (*scores 1/5*)

The number one reason your business exists is to make money. Mission statements simply enshrine the requirement to deliver shareholder value.

First **steps** …

If you estimate your organization is poor at this start by:

1. Calling together the founder/CEO, other key decision-makers, people who have been in the business a long time (from whatever role, cleaner to director). Ask them what they think the Purpose, the Why, of the business is? If you get immediate consensus go to step 4. If not go to step 2.

2. Run a workshop investigating: What it is about your organization that attracted individuals to work there? Why they chose it over others? What is it about the organization that they particularly believe in? Which bits of what it does or offers would they not want to lose? Include an exercise in which you consider a scenario in which you have lost the brand and have to start from scratch: What is important to you? Where does this brand start from? What is it going to do? What is it going to be about? What do you believe about it? What could others believe?

3. As and when you achieve a shared belief – sense-check it against business needs.

4. Using your "Purpose" as a guide, list the things you do which align with it and the things that don't.

5. Stop doing the things that don't. Create additional activities which do.

chapter 2 Open Capital

／ Definition

Using crowd-funding platforms or principles to raise capital through micro-investments.

In the final analysis the most significant disruption changing the way organizations function and business is done is likely to be in the role capital has to play.

That's why Open Capital is our second Principle of Open Business.

In line with the needs of the industrial age, capital was organized on the principles of mass and centralized control; big blocks of cash held by small groups of decision-makers fitted that world.

But the networked world requires something new: something which delivers faster decisions together with wider distribution of both risk and reward; something which moves the role of the customer from "end user" to participant and partner; something which is a better fit with networks.

We call this something Open Capital: Using crowd-funding platforms or principles to raise capital through micro-investments.

We see example after example of crowd-funding platforms emerging (e.g., Kickstarter, Seedrs, Grow VC) and success upon success in their support for new products and services which Big Capital could not or would not support.

But today's entrepreneurs opt for Open Capital knowing that the advantages go far beyond a new route to capital.

Open Capital shares the costs and risks and therefore the ownership and the passion. It democratizes innovation. And this is valuable to organizations old and new.

The wins are in:

- Lowering the cost and risk of innovation. Fairphone (which we will return to in the chapter on Transparency) was structured around a plan to put its unique smartphone into production only when it had secured around 1.5m in euros through their own internal crowd-funding process.
- De-risking innovation. By providing a "money-where-your-mouth-is" proof of concept that a Facebook Like or a Twitter Retweet can't hope to match, generating a pre-sales order book validating that there is a market: TikTok watch is an example of this. Traditional routes to capital had failed to find a backer for this innovative iPod nano/watch. More than 13,000 individual backers put their money where their mouth was on Kickstarter (the crowd-funding website) to prove old capital wrong. Those putting up the cash wanted the watch so provided the funds – supply and demand in perfect unison.
- Priming a platform of advocates ahead of launch to provide a peer-to-peer marketing launch – as seen in the examples of Fairphone, TikTok and NearDesk (of which more shortly).
- Connecting lenders to the market with greater accuracy – something the subprime lending crisis of 2007 (and its impact) revealed as sadly lacking in traditional models – for example, Prosper.com has now funded $750m in personal loans in peer-to-peer models.
- Opening up your innovation process early to benefit from all of the above.

- Democratizing innovation. Providing a real sense of ownership for those taking part.
- Enabling niche innovation to scale. Open Capital affordably and efficiently enables organizations of all sizes to test, develop, and deliver to niche need.

Peer-funded partnerships also offer the opportunity to create value beyond the back slap in the boardroom and the bottom line on the balance sheet; value creation which acknowledges resources are finite, that people, communities, societies, and ecologies are connected and matter to each other.

And this in itself provides a genuine competitive advantage that the wisest global entrepreneurs are quick to identify. As Sir Richard Branson puts it in his book *Screw Business As Usual* (Virgin Books 2013): "the boundaries between work and higher purpose are merging into one – where doing good really is good for business."

In a connected world, where to win is to work together with ever greater numbers of people who care about the same things you do, few are going to sign up to support businesses which are damaging the ecosystem in which they exist – let alone support those organizations with their own money. Open Capital will therefore be a key driver of "doing good is good for business."

Tom Ball is a good example of the new breed of entrepreneur who has turned to Open Capital not as a lender of last resort, but because he believed it would give him a positive competitive advantage.

When he turned to Seedrs in pursuit of crowd-funding he did so with a view to testing the appetite of the market for his product, circumventing the demands of big investors, and creating a ready-made team of marketers for the product: people who were prepared to put their money where their mouth was.

There are no fools waiting to be parted from their money on Seedrs. Every new applicant is exposed to a stringent test to see if they understand the risks involved and how share-holding works. No one is allowed to invest more than a small percentage of their disposable income (which Seedrs assesses you for).

It really is a test. Fail the online assessment and the platform won't let you invest. In short it takes the traditional "investments can go down as well as up" small print of the mainstream financial sector and not only writes it large, it pretty much rams it down your throat. No one can say they didn't know the risks. No one can say they had been fooled.

In the UK those wishing to invest have another advantage: since April 2012 the Seed Enterprise Investment Scheme (SEIS) offers huge tax reliefs to investors who buy new shares in the early days of the life of a company. SEIS is among the most generous tax-relief schemes available to UK taxpayers.

Unfortunately almost no other country offers such significant support for investors in start-ups.

Seedrs is also (at time of writing) the only crowd-funding platform in the UK to have FSA approval though others are queuing up behind.

So the bar is set high on getting investment on Seedrs. Even so, Tom's NearDesk broke three records (raising the most, having the most number of investors, and raising the money fastest) when it went live on the site, raising over £150,000 of series one funding from 139 investors putting up between £10 and £50,000 each.

You may be concerned that this high a number of people who may feel they now have skin in Tom's game could lead to a "too many cooks" spoiling of the broth of monumental proportions. Not at all.

Seedrs acts as a nominee for all the investors, performing the basic due diligence – checking the veracity of Tom's claims in his pitch and holding him to account. But neither Seedrs nor the investors are banging on Tom's door every day as he tries to grow his business. They don't sit on the board and they don't get voting rights. Management by grand committee is avoided and the fleet-footedness of a start-up guaranteed.

So why have so many people backed Tom? NearDesk is just the latest in a series of ventures for him. But perhaps it is the one that matters most to him.

It is a business with a Purpose (see Chapter 1). Tom hates needless commuting – it takes us out of our communities, it costs us time with our families and it's bad for the environment, he argues. It is something he sees as wrong with the world which he would like to try to put right.

NearDesk is an attempt to get all commuters to work just one day a week nearer to home by providing access to appropriate workspaces.

"We're more like Expedia than the Hilton Hotel," explains Tom.

Funnily enough when he suggests to companies the idea of their staff working one day a week closer to home, they often counter with, "perhaps two would be better," he claims.

As well they may. The average cost of a desk in central London is now running at approximately £15,000 a year. Hot-desking doesn't solve the problem; it just moves it around, says Tom.

He expands: "52% of most companies' carbon foot-print is made up of the commute by its staff."

In total Tom argues it can cost a corporate more to own a desk than they are paying the employee sat at it.

"Owning desks and buildings has become a core competency for many companies. It's fascinating to challenge that and ask questions about the nature or need to own today," he says.

He's passionate about wanting people to spend more time in the communities in which they live. "If you aren't getting home until nine at night you can't use your local shops, you have to go to the Tesco's and Sainsbury's. If you are working locally you can shop locally, have lunch locally," he says.

And as many fathers and mothers will recognize there is another aspect to commuting which disrupts the lives we would rather lead.

"When commuting you are usually up and out of the house before your children wake, and home after they have gone to sleep," he adds.

All of which means Tom is a driven man, a man on a mission – a man with a purpose which his company can make reality.

"Needless commuting drives me nuts. There's a bundle of benefits from reducing commuting and increasing community."

Open Capital, says Tom, felt like the right tool to do the job of funding a purpose-driven venture. "This is a campaign, not just a vehicle to make money. So crowd-funding felt like the right thing to do – in a by-the-people-for-the-people sense."

It's that Purpose that has drawn in the investors, set the records, and which was still there when round two of funding raised a further £50,000 of funding in September 2013.

The biggest benefit, says Tom, has been the advocates Open Capital has created to join him on the mission.

the biggest benefit ... has been the advocates

"A stupidly simple example; when the first round of funding closed, Seedrs put out a tweet about the success of Neardesk (on Twitter.com). It was retweeted five times in the next hour. I know that two of those tweeting were investors and suspect the other three were, too."

The advocacy was live and growing.

"We have advocates out there and almost every day one of our investors will ping us something useful, or introduce us to someone who can help," says Tom.

He has scaled his business – every investor feels part of it and is out there helping it succeed.

"We have 139 people out there who, some way or another, are part of the team. Effectively, we have people paying us to be on the team. It was very, very nice to be given the additional reassurance that others felt the idea was worth backing. The average invested was £1000."

Most people putting in cash were doing so at significantly lower sums than even angel investors (typically those who provide seed funds in the £100k–£1m bracket). But understanding the angel community gives us a clue as to the motivations involved here.

Tom explains: "There's been some research into why people make angel investments and the number one reason is not to make money, it's to (my words) have something to talk about at dinner parties."

Purpose, or belief, is surely an element of this in today's Open Business.

Tom describes it as: "I've got spare money, I'll invest 90 per cent of it in the Prudential and put the rest of it in things I believe in that can change the world. Why have money if you can't do something interesting with it?"

In short, Open Capital is a way in which we can all strive to make businesses that make the world a little better, more than make a quick buck. We are using our own cash to help make the things that we believe in happen.

Tom makes the point that loads of people making small investments are also likely to make longer bets than those who swoop in with "needle moving" amounts of cash with the adherent pressures to deliver rapid returns.

The result will be capital aligned with things that people passionately believe in – with their Purpose.

It opens the ability to make change with capital to everyone. You don't have to be an entrepreneur. You can support change with a small risk to your own finances rather than throwing in your day job and trying to open (for example) a vegan supermarket.

"For the entrepreneur, the small investment is lovely, but what's really important is getting someone else on the team who believes," says Tom.

For Tom, Open Capital is a very powerful and alluring alternative to the VC (venture capitalist) model. It's faster too.

"If I want to get a VC to invest I have to play this silly game of getting more than one of them to want to. They don't want to be the 'only mug in town'.

"And if we had a VC invest, we'd be fighting with them from day one because they have all these control rights."

Far from making his business look "way out there" to traditional investors, Tom believes the Open Capital model has validated it for them.

"They have no omnipotent way of knowing what to back. In a way, the fact that the market (through Seedrs.com) has validated Neardesk, has given them a steer to potential success they might otherwise not have had.

"In fact, within an hour of the first round of funding closing, one of the most respected investors in Europe got in touch to express interest. We had three or four VCs approach us off the back of it."

Since Seedrs (as the name suggests) is just for seed funding, VCs aren't threatened by it – but they would do well, suggests Tom, to keep an eye on it to guide their later stage investment.

"The thing I love about Open Capital," says Tom, "is that we are all now potential investors. And there are more of us investing £10 than there are investing £100,000."

NearDesk – at time of writing – operates just one test venue in Kings Cross, London. But 50 more are live but not yet being promoted. By the time of publication that network should be expanding still further.

One of the reasons it will expand is that the business operates as a platform, seeking partnership with others who can make the mission happen – whether they look like potential rivals or not.

Tom plans to create a data map of supply and demand for the requirements of NearDesk. His ambition is to take an Open Data approach to this and share it with whoever can make best use of it – a clear sign of his belief in the journey.

"That's how we can help the whole industry succeed," he said.

As we said before, NearDesk is just the latest in a series of ventures for Tom. Crucially it is one driven by Purpose.

"Have a purpose, something to motivate – the money will follow," he says.

To take advantage of the principles of Open Business, Tom has some advice:

"Companies need to make a body language change. They need to stop clutching things to their chests and start walking around with their palms open. They'll gain more than they lose by being open."

* * *

Jouko Ahvenainen has a background in analytics, technology, and mobile.

His Twitter profile (you'll find him there as @jahven) states that he created the world's first social-network analytics tool (Xtract) and now focuses on new peer-to-peer investment models; that's Grow VC.

"We started about three years ago as a funding service for start-ups. We aimed to be global from the start and I think we are still the only platform of our type to operate very globally."

As well as building start-ups he has been an investor in start-ups. Much of what Grow VC is was born out of his frustrations and a desire to democratize the ability to invest in start-ups.

"We felt the start-up funding model didn't work so well. If I start with the definition of a good market, there has to be enough demand and supply and all information to all parties. Traditionally the start-up funding model is quite far away from that.

"It's often based on limited information, driven by personal or local contacts or networks and it has been dominated in many places by 'important' VCs.

"We came to the conclusion that to get the market more open, more transparent and more effective makes sense for companies but also for investors," says Jouko.

"The idea was to get more capital for start-up companies but also to open the opportunity for anybody to invest in start-ups."

For investors the idea was to give them the opportunity to compare more investment options – choosing from a larger numbers of start-ups than ordinarily available.

"When I first became an investor I would have to rely on people making introductions to companies for me. I would see the first start-up and think 'wow, that's a great opportunity, I should invest here.' Then I would see the next start-up and think 'wow, that's an even better opportunity.'" he says.

How could he know he was being exposed to *all* the best opportunities for him?

The transparency required of those using his platform goes some way to correcting that. Widening choice for investors (5000+ companies have used Grow VC) helps too.

The other correction Grow VC strives to make is to the supply side of the monetary equation. Today the platform has around 20,000 people globally ready to invest.

One early beneficiary was Australian company Cintep which had come up with a design for a water-saving shower. There are obvious advantages for this in an arid climate. And for anyone with large water bills. Hotel chains, for example.

"It recycles something like 80% of the water," said Jouko.

They were able to raise the first $100,000 from the Grow VC service. After that they have done very well, winning clean tech awards, additional funding and (yes) deals with hotel chains, he says.

So why did they opt to raise funds through the crowd?

"The Australian Venture Capital ecosystem doesn't work so well. It's very difficult to get VC money," says Jouko.

"They also said that many VCs who would invest focus on Internet and software services – not so much in a company with an innovation product idea.

"The Kickstarter model also doesn't work for them. They needed the funding to develop a product. They weren't ready to deliver the product to those people who invest. They really needed equity investment," he adds.

Jouko's career has taken him around the globe. Starting out from Finland he has lived and worked in the Far East, the US, and now London. Before taking to the serial entrepreneur life he held senior positions in companies including Nokia, Sonera, Cap Gemini, and Ernst & Young.

He's seen the challenges to his dream across the world. They have resulted in Grow VC Group having entities based in the US, the UK, and Hong Kong.

"Making this work across the globe has been legally complex. In the US for example the whole area has been heavily regulated. Ordinary people aren't allowed to invest in private companies."

In this and other ways, Jouko wanted to improve on the way the venture capital market works.

With three years' experience in the Open Capital market, Grow VC Group has started to develop other elements to its business which are linked to the same principle.

The first is a consulting and investment banking service in which Grow VC acts as advisor to companies investing in start-ups but also in setting up local crowd-funding ecosystems around the world.

This approach suits the way scaling works in the world of Open. The Grow VC idea is also being distributed widely as a platform – Crowd Valley – to support those who could and should benefit from it.

"We help others start-up their own platforms," says Jouko.

Crowd Valley provides the platform and back office services for crowd-funding, peer-to-peer investing, and alternative asset marketplaces for securities pros. Grow VC remains an international equity marketplace for early-stage ventures to connect with a global audience of entrepreneurs, funders, and experts.

The Crowd Valley platform is offered as a software-as-a-service solution. Jouko explains:

"Companies or local organizations can easily create their own crowd-funding with our platform. Many incubators, universities or local business groups want to start locally. We take care of the platform and all the back office functionality for transactions and investment tracking."

He says he now has partners who use Grow VC for funding later-phase companies, commodities, real estate, and energy resources.

For Jouko the back office functions are critical in crowd-funding models which go beyond the Kickstarter concept.

Kickstarter is one of the better known crowd-funding platforms. It can claim many successes in launching new products which may not otherwise have seen the light of day.

But Jouko makes the point that it's a relatively simple model more aligned with buying than buying into.

"In Kickstarter the whole process is over when the company gets your money (you get the product you have effectively funded the production of in return).

"In investment and equity crowd-funding it's only the starting point when the money has been collected. Then you must handle all the securities and the settlement of the investment and after that keep track of the investments and report on them. The complexities of this kind of investment are much higher than the Kickstarter model. We have tried to make a very simple platform to enable that." he said.

There are now 500 organizations using the platform in this way.

Grow VC Group has also started working on co-investment models with partners.

"We have seen that to get crowd funding to work we must make it work with other investors. For example if there is a start-up with real potential, it's good to get investors who can make follow up, second and third round investments."

The platform works a little like a LinkedIn for start-ups – offering a place for them to develop their profile, report their milestones, and provide (to investors) a scorecard against which they can be measured over time and against other opportunities.

"We do this because I believe that the only way to measure start-ups is in their execution capability. Their ideas, or even their teams, are not enough," said Jouko.

He also believes one of the key impacts of improving the connections between investors and companies is in the ability to start smaller and grow less in leaps and bounds and more organically.

start smaller and grow ... more organically

"Now they can get a small amount of money, show what they can do with that, and then really go step by step with small increments of money. The traditional model has been that many companies try to get as much money as they can as early as possible, because it is so complex and time consuming (especially for key people in a business) to do."

By reducing the complexity, cost and time, Grow VC reduces the amounts needed to right-size chunks to meet actual short-term requirements: little and often (if successful) vs large and rare (in case you aren't).

That in itself is a better fit with the niches of the web.

It's not just individuals who are using the platform. Some firms are now trying it as their route into innovation via the funding of start-ups.

"Some corporates are modeling using it internally to try to link up the corporate venture activity with departmental needs. Often corporate ventures end up living their own lives with little link to current departments," he says.

Jouko continues: "We have been seeking cooperative models through which they can support each other. Basically, we can create an internal crowd-funding inside the organisation."

"We see that the most important part now, for Grow VC Group, is to build a kind of bridge between the new crowd and peer-to-peer models and the traditional finance sector.

"It is crucial for the new models to be integrated with other investment models. The traditional investment world is very keen to be linked to the new models. We are already working with many investment companies, investment banks and investors."

Some institutional investors are interested in running crowd-funding models with automated triggers built in to speed up decision-making.

"If a case meets their criteria, and the company hits (for example) 50% of its target funding from the crowd, an alert could place this directly into the institutional co-investors evaluation process," he explains.

"Within a few hours they would be able to decide if they will give the other 50%."

While Jouko cannot name the companies involved due to the early stage of development, one thing is certain, Open Capital within the enterprise has arrived.

This final disruption promises to be more fundamental than the disruption to the business of content creation and distribution, more disruptive even than our ability to self-organize to shape what we care about.

It is a significant accelerator of change.

Now we can self-organize to fund what we care about. That disrupts the mass, centralized blocks of capital model we know and switches us to one of widely-distributed ownership and leadership.

The web has been like a Big Bang to "business as usual" – disrupting media, marketing, customer service, new product development, the business of elections, the business of who governs us, how we are educated, how we are cared for, and so much more.

But disruption of this people-power kind alone has its limits. Even though we can find other people who care about the same things as we do, and in so doing lower the cost of action to achieve the shared purposes we have, long-lasting and valuable change is slowed by the huge inertia of Big Capital.

There are those who argue Big Capital is just too big to be undone from the edge. But who thought the arrival of the Internet would one day herald the end of Big Media? Today in the UK more people read Twitter each morning than read all the national newspapers put together. The power shift is almost complete in media; the content and distribution monopolies gone.

And so for Big Capital?

Make no mistake, Big Capital is holding back real change. Take Facebook …

Big Capital is holding back real change

First the VCs have to get paid.

"You haven't developed a business model to meet the needs of the networked world? Tough luck! Pay me!" And so we get traditional broadcast-style ads interrupting your time on Facebook.

Then the VCs are replaced by Big Capital. Who want dividends. Fast. No time to develop a new model. "You've caught all those fish in a barrel – let's go spear them …"

Where is the interest in long-term benefit to the users? To their communities? To their society?

New York University professor and author Clay Shirky has a nice line about news websites which are "designed as if the web exists."

We must make businesses which are designed as if the world – as it actually is – exists.

Exploitation which damages our connected well-being has never been welcome. The fact is that exploitation is visible now more than it ever has been before: The web has revealed our interconnectedness like nothing in history.

exploitation is visible now more than it ever has been

And that is a genie which is not going back in its bottle.

Change will come; Big Capital inertia can only slow things. And where we are frustrated, where we care most, where we see the most significant damage to our future and to that of those we care about, we will vote with our connectedness, our collaboration, our action – and now with our personal funds.

We'll chip away at first – Kickstarter by Kickstarter – but one day Big Capital will wake up to find itself in the place newspapers have.

How realistic is that? How soon can we imagine the old mass, centralized model of capital ceding to this edge-led open approach?

Andrew Hill has worked for the London-based *Financial Times* for a quarter of a century. His current role as management editor (and associate editor) sees him investigating and challenging emerging and traditional business models. He has regular access to the world's leading CEOs and their senior teams.

Andrew has already seen large organizations use "play money" for internal crowd-funding of ideas which a corporation will use to identify the best-supported ideas and which they will then back with real money.

"I've seen this done with Citigroup, for example. They'll use this to identify projects for innovation. But the problem with more strait-laced companies is that they don't really want to share the idea externally.

"If you are a bank looking for the next big idea you are going to be wary about letting anyone else get sight of that," he warns. "It's easier to consumer test an idea than to gain investment in it, essentially because investors want more information."

Opening your idea for investment means, potentially, larger investors could chip in at low levels simply to get a view of what is coming next from the company seeking investment, he argues.

"It's a risk for big companies that I'm not convinced many would be prepared to run, right now."

But Andrew can see how those large businesses which invest in start-ups to give themselves an innovation advantage may start to see Open Capital as an opportunity to reverse engineer their current approach. So rather than investing in start-ups, large businesses could crowd-fund their own ideas – internalizing the innovation.

This does not suit every kind of organization. The banks, for example, with their regulation of control, are hampered. But, Andrew agrees, they are also at greatest risk from the Open Capital model.

"If you think of the ultimate kind of crowd-funding – Google going around Wall Street for its IPO, for example, the banks of course hate that. They are very keen to maintain their lock-hold on the ultimate funding of IPOs," says Andrew.

The question is can they hold on? In a networked economy in which little by little individuals back the smaller-scale things they believe in – do we need the large-scale solutions?

We should expect the network of the web to deliver niche, long-tail solutions, yet we find ourselves facing giant almost-monopolies time and time again – Google, Facebook, YouTube, Twitter, Amazon, to name those dominant in the West.

One reason for this is that large companies work very hard to adapt – to maintain their dominance, says Andrew. He believes crowd-funding alone won't be enough to end the dominance of scale – but it does open a huge new middle ground.

crowd-funding alone won't ... end the dominance of scale

"Open Capital may serve something which is a venture with a purpose. It may not be in the 'I want to be the next Twitter' category and therefore it may not need the level of capital that Twitter needed. It will be the kind of organization that people will want to be involved with – but it may not deliver the next Tesco, for example," says Andrew.

"It doesn't knock the props away from the big corporate," Andrew concludes.

Our challenge to that is if you have all the middle scale served by Open Capital, and you were able to meet all needs in this way – with all the attendant support of people backing ideas they cared about – would you still need the big guys?

"The big companies, the smart ones anyway, are capable of change – using what they have and the principles of networked organizations that others can access. They may not go as fast.

"A Facebook of the size it is today may not develop as fast or as innovatively as when it was a dorm-room idea, but I think that it still has the capacity to do so.

"What is interesting about the crowd-funding idea, as you describe it, is that it can open up some middle ground for people to develop something that doesn't need to go from 0–60 in two seconds, but can be gradually developed," says Andrew.

We believe that's an important contributor in building businesses which are more meaningful for those who create them, fund them, work for them, and buy from them. These are businesses with a more human scale – and they may prove to be a better fit with the niche, connected world the web reveals than the mass industrial world we are leaving behind.

The current and repeating drift toward mass that the web has delivered so far is not a necessary truth. The web is still young.

For example, the upload and download speeds of your Internet access are almost certainly skewed toward broadcast. You can download much faster than you can upload. That has an impact on the roles we feel we play – as participants or passive receivers. It drives how much effort we will put into participating.

Open Capital is where, right now and despite that skew, people are prepared to go beyond just sharing digital content to support what they believe in. It is where they raise their level of participation to put a little bit of money behind what they believe in as well.

Imagine how many more of us may do the same when more of us feel even more like genuine participants?

Summary

Open Capital uses crowd-funding platforms or principles to raise capital through micro-investments. It shares the costs and risks and therefore the ownership and the passion. It funds things people want.

G O A L   S T A T E / W O R S T   C A S E

Where does your business stand from 1 to 5?

Goal state (*scores 5/5*)

The organization is 100% crowd-funded.

Worst case (*scores 1/5*)

All funding comes from "Big Capital" – VCs, institutional shareholders – concentrating power over the organization and its aims in those institutions.

First **steps** …

If you estimate your organization is poor at this start by:

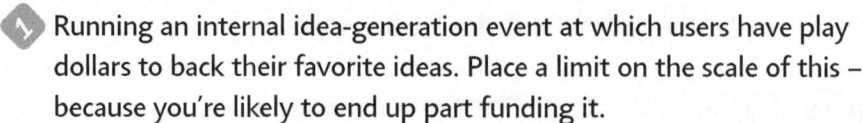 Running an internal idea-generation event at which users have play dollars to back their favorite ideas. Place a limit on the scale of this – because you're likely to end up part funding it.

2 Run the winning idea on your preferred crowd-funding platform (or if you have access to the right audience, on your own platform) and commit to providing half the funding if the crowd will match the rest by pre-ordering the output.

3 Limit this initial test to pre-ordering in the Kickstarter model rather than equity stake in the Grow VC model.

4 Should the test succeed, consider how you could offer equity in future projects to people outside of your business.

chapter 3

Networked Organization

/ Definition

The organization functions as a platform connecting internal networks to the external for a common Purpose.

Our third Principle is one that defines the organizational structure of an Open Business. It is that it should be a Networked Organization. The organization functions as a platform connecting internal networks to external ones for a common Purpose (see Chapter 1).

This speaks to and supports our primary definition of an Open Business: One which uses its resources to bring people together to achieve a shared Purpose – designed from the outset to scale through participation, making partners of customers.

This approach to the organization, sometimes alternatively described as the "platform organization," is now widely accepted and advocated, even by traditional management consultancies.

For example McKinsey defines today's most successful organizations as "the Networked Enterprise."

Jacques Burghin and Michael Chui reported in December 2010's *Mckinsey Quarterly*:

> 27 percent of the companies in our survey reported having both market share gains against their competitors and higher profit margins ... with earnings growing faster than the rest. Highly networked enterprises were 50 percent more likely to fall in this high-performance group than other organizations. This finding suggests that the fully networked enterprise could become the benchmark for more vigorous competition in many industries.
>
> Moreover, the benefits from the use of collaborative technologies at fully networked organisations appear to be multiplicative in nature: these enterprises seem to be "learning organisations" in which lessons from interacting with one set of stakeholders in turn improve the ability to realise value in interactions with others. If this hypothesis is correct, competitive advantage at these companies will accelerate as network effects kick in, network connections become richer, and learning cycles speed up.

Why be a Networked Organization?

The key business benefits of the Networked Organization are that it:

- Links people and teams – breaking down conventional boundaries (e.g., departments and geographies)
- Offers pragmatic, rapid, and efficient scaling through access to a global workforce of niche skills
- De-risks/removes the threat of over capacity
- Brings the organization closer to both market and customer – since it integrates with both
- Maximizes the knowledge potential and flow of an enterprise
- Offers greater resilience, minimizing the threat and impact of disruption
- Enables both responsiveness and adaptability in a way more rigid and siloed organizational structures can't match

Apple may not present much of an externally networked face to the world (it is notoriously secretive – indeed its corporate PR machine refused to put up any currently serving senior executive for interview for this book) but its approach to scaling the functional ability of its iPhone and iPad has been exceptionally networked – and exceptionally successful.

Apple resources provided a platform to enable those outside the organization (developers, brands, media companies) to create value by building, marketing, and selling apps (typically to make iPhones and iPads more useful to their owners). The app makers get 70% of the sales value on each download made via the App Store.

By taking this networked approach Apple can service the long tail of need without carrying the risk of employing factories full of developers trying to guestimate the total potential functional requirements of every single iPhone and iPad purchaser on Earth.

service the long tail of need without carrying the risk

It enables near-endless owner-selected customization and personalization of its products. Customers get phones and tablets that do what they want them to do, software entrepreneurs get a ready market for their innovations, and Apple gets …? Well, Apple estimates the App Store's contribution to market capitalization value as of December 2011 was ITRO $7.08bn.

Organizations which aren't preparing to adapt to take advantage of the networked approach may, according to IBM, find themselves in a minority in a few short years. In a survey conducted in May 2012, it found that more than half of the questioned CEOs (53%) were planning to use technology to facilitate greater partnering and collaboration with outside organizations, while 52% were shifting their attention to promoting greater internal collaboration. In 2008, slightly more than half of the CEOs interviewed planned to partner extensively. Now, more than two-thirds intend to do so.

We have been thinking, writing, and delivering on this shift from traditional to networked (or platform) organizations for more than half a decade. As more tech gets deployed, the clearer the requirement to connect inside and out reveals itself.

In many respects the arrival of 3D printing lifts the veil on the true role of the organization – suggesting a platform (or networked) approach has been the natural state to which organizations were always going to return when our view became clear.

When we talk about means of production, we often think about the machinery to produce. But that does not mean the device.

In a mass production world the connection between the machinery and the process is clearer. Traditionally, a newspaper owner needed to own a printing press. They also needed to employ a team of writers, photographers, editors, and so on to produce the content. Which was the means of production? The printing press or the producers of the content? The two were so tightly connected it didn't matter.

On the web, the owner of the means of production of content is the person who creates the content. In reality this was always so. In the past the owner of the means of production of content had no access to the printing press. Now they have (or at least they have access to its equivalent in the form of the web – where, of course, everyone has the option to be a publisher).

The same is true of factories, where the production line is the equivalent of the printing press. In a world in which everyone has access to their own production line (a home 3D printer) the real means of production is revealed as those coming up with the ideas, process, and required designs.

3D printing reveals the need for organizations to think of themselves far less as the makers of, and far more the supporters of the makers of, "their" products.

* * *

Philip Letts comes from a long line of innovators. His family came up with the world's first paperback diary a little over 200 years ago and built a media empire on its success.

Identifying a need and moving to meet it with the best tools for the job must be in the blood because Philip is now running a platform built to take advantage of an increasingly networked world.

Not only is his business, blur Group, a Networked Organization, it provides the platform to create thousands more.

In our Goal State definition of a Networked Organization we suggest no more than one in ten of your ecosystem should be employees of your own business.

Philip says his business is "off the scale" by that definition with 50 employees serving a network of 30,000 or more in 141 countries.

"We are providing an enabling platform for others to use as well as for ourselves," says Philip. Around 1200 new businesses a month are joining.

Philip's way of thinking was arrived at as a result of a journey from traditional media through digital disruption.

He was brought up in the family media business and took charge of a part of the business where technology, publishing, and education combined in the late 1980s: CMI.

CMI became one of the first European businesses to be on the web in 1993 and was eventually sold to Gartner Group.

Philip moved on to run a series of technology businesses. One did corporate portals.

"If you think about one of the earliest visions for corporate portals, it was to enable more networked organizations – that was kind of the idea," says Philip.

Then Philip became involved with business-to-business exchanges.

"B2B exchanges are very networked in their organization. They are about building and enabling both the supply and demand side in a specific industry vertical.

"Working in the sector taught me and my teams much more about this concept of an open network/ecosystem which could behave a bit like a vertical micro-economy," says Philip.

Before long he was asked to run a large B2B exchange in California. "That was interesting because it was about networking together tens of thousands of businesses worldwide."

Piece by piece the jigsaw for blur Group was coming together.

"We were helping them to do business together through cash and barter. It was really while I was running that, that I started developing the ideas around blur Group," he explained.

"The original vision was that as technology becomes more pervasive and utilitarian – and broadband gets wider and wider and wider, every organization will become more connected up to others.

"As that happens organizational structures are likely to change."

Philip wanted to build an enabling platform to support that, online and in the cloud. But in what sector?

"We decided that what moves the needle in businesses is services."

The result is blur Group – a global expert service exchange. It connects businesses with more than 32,000 expert service providers in more than 140 countries around the world.

The technology was built 2006–2007 and the suppliers attracted to the platform 2007–2009. The team started to bring buyers to it in 2009.

Expert providers are organized into service areas: design (including advertising, apps and website, product and print, and video); marketing (including customer acquisition, strategy, PR, and campaign management); content (including copywriting, online content, print, and technical writing); art (including 3D, photography, and street art); innovation (IP, licensing, ideation); technology (apps, data, software, etc.); legal (B2B, employment, financial, franchising, property); and accounting (including financial planning and reporting, and modeling).

Buyers – those an agency may call clients – include the likes of HSBC, The FT, Paddy Power, GE Healthcare, and Butlins to name just a few.

Customers submit a brief online for a service or a project by filling out the platform's own briefing app. It takes them through all the questions they need to answer to create a successful brief. The brief then gets listed on the exchange and the trading platform then takes them through all the stages of managing a project.

The system narrows the options for the buyer to six or seven potential suppliers (the number of responses received often reaches into the mid-20s). The customer then filters down to two or three pitches – all done online.

If required, customers are welcome to hold physical meetings. But Philip says it has been fascinating to watch the desire for, and evidence of, physical meetings falling away over the last four or five years.

Once a supplier is selected payment systems then kick in. The platform also supports review processes and online discussion forums as additional measures to support quality.

The suppliers are paid by blur Group, the buyer pays blur Group – thus removing the challenge for many new or niche players in all the administration surrounding attaining that first payment order from a client.

The platform makes a margin of a minimum of 20% – healthy in the typical agency model.

Even if the project requires multiple suppliers, the buyer is only dealing with one vendor – the platform.

The business makes some ancillary revenues – some listing fees for customers and a recently launched premium account which delivers transactional data and multi-user environments for larger players, but it is the share it takes for acting as platform that delivers the vast majority of its revenues.

They are far from small time, too. The company is now listed on the London Stock Exchange and is targeting revenues of £8.7m in 2013 with ambitions to double that in 2014. It was forecasted to break even at the end of 2013 and go into profit in 2014.

The largest brief so far delivered through the platform was worth $5m.

Is this evidence of an idea in tune with the world as it actually is today?

a more efficient way for businesses to both communicate and transact

"We genuinely felt there had to be a more efficient way for businesses to both communicate and transact with each other. Services to us seemed a natural area to tackle. Businesses spend more on services than they do almost anything else (in terms of external costs).

"We felt the whole way businesses interact in the B2B world has always been a little archaic, they hadn't really moved to an online model and as a result it isn't an open, meritocratic environment. It's an environment driven by who you know, how big you are, and all that kind of stuff."

Philip believes that as the world becomes more digital and more niche and more global the old models no longer work. The networked approach meets this increasing democratization of business.

He notes that there are huge global players, mid-size regional ones, and millions of small local providers.

"We thought if we could put a platform in the middle of all that then both the buyers and the sellers would be able to operate much more efficiently and get those cost efficiencies.

"We've all been buyers and we all recognized the inefficiencies and wanted to do something about it."

If businesses weren't interested in being more open in the way they operate, in being more open to external services and resources, blur Group would not be able to exist, says Philip. It certainly wouldn't be scaling the way it is.

Philip sees the Networked Organization as an essential principle for businesses of all sizes.

"Small businesses can now scale faster because they need fewer full-time internal resources because they can tap into things like our platform to be more networked.

"Medium-sized businesses can become less regional and more global. And large businesses can restructure themselves."

So why does blur Group employ anyone? For the same reason that any Networked Organization will always retain a central team – to deliver against its core competencies.

That splits into three areas for blur Group: technology (the nuts and bolts of the digital platform itself), sales and marketing (to continue to build the ecosystem), and customer support (to educate and support their customers in becoming more networked organizations).

Given that blur Group uses its own platform to service its own needs whenever possible, what is Philip's criteria for retaining the skills in-house – for having a full-time employee?

"That's a very good question. Our employees run programs both internally and externally. As a result of this shift to a more networked organization one of the most important skills for everyone across the business is project management.

"If you are going to have a more networked organization that means you are going to be managing more resources that are external than internal.

"And as we all know, that takes really good co-ordination skills."

The question is, at what point does the energy expended in that become so great that you bring the task back into the center? As technology improves, as the friction in the communications reduces, that point gets further and further away.

Measuring that point – through productivity, return per employee, etc. – becomes increasingly valuable in the Networked Organization.

"With these models you become more metrics focused. We have one person in our business who spends all of their time – 100% – worrying about internal metrics. We are constantly measuring the ROI on every resource that we have – every employee on the team."

For Philip the role of full-time employees is very clear. Beyond a handful of extremely focused core competencies, they become an enabling and supporting platform for those doing the business of the organization outside what used to be regarded as its walls.

"In the end this shift to the Networked Organization means companies have to ask themselves some big questions," says Philip.

"If you have 1000 employees, ask yourself, 'could we deliver the same with 300 employees with more service providers networked into those – and how long would it take us to shift to that and who would be able to help us make that change?'

"We – as a platform provider – want to see more advisors, more organizational change consultants, more strategic consultants, starting to talk to businesses about how you move from the traditional command and control model – with lots of internal resources, firewalls, and real estate – lots of internal cost – and shift to a much more fluid, networked business.

"Who helps you make that change? There's not enough out there to help. This book could make the difference. What it's trying to achieve is great."

Summary

A Networked Organization focuses on its core competencies while enabling and supporting mutually beneficial activity outside the organization. It offers small- to medium-sized organizations the opportunity to operate on a global scale. Companies of all sizes can reduce internal costs and risks.

GOAL STATE / WORST CASE

Where does your business stand from 1 to 5?

Goal state (*scores 5/5*)

No more than 1 in 10 in your organization's ecosystem are employees – the rest partner with you from outside the organization. Your staff act as an enabling platform for participation from outside the organization.

Worst case (*scores 1/5*)

You employ staff to fulfill every function of the enterprise.

First **steps** ...

If you estimate your organization is poor at this start by asking:

1. What are your core competencies?
2. Outside of these – what are your staff doing?
3. How could you support those outside of your organization to achieve similar results?
4. Who can help you make that shift, who do you need to help you make it?
5. When will you start making the change?

$\Large 4$

chapter

Shareability

Definition

Packaging knowledge for easy and open sharing both internally and externally.

Sharing is the cultural key to collaboration. It is where the organizational design principles of collaboration reside.

It is a principle which has the powerful benefit of flattening hierarchies, distributing responsibility, and making the organization more strategy and goal led than management and task directed.

Shareability:

- Taps into peer-to-peer distribution networks, reducing the cost of marketing and improving targeting. Our friends know best what we value. They don't share with us what they don't think we'll like. If they do their reputation with us diminishes. It costs them to get this wrong. When O'Reilly removed the DRM anti-sharing mechanism on its e-books it saw their sales rise 104% within a year. Friends did the marketing to friends (source: BoingBoing.com).

- Raises the organization's thought leadership profile. Helen Clegg, knowledge team director at AT Kearney, says the global management consultancy has started a series of podcasts (downloadable audio content) and made it available to all via their site and on iTunes. The podcasts share knowledge externally on globalization, sustainability, and the latest trends in procurement. Wikis, social-media-led team sites, and webinars have also been deployed at AT Kearney.
- Breaks down internal silos and external barriers – by providing the social objects (the expression of ideas, concepts, goals, challenges, beliefs, and other conversation starters) around which collaboration is inspired. This means a shared purpose, need, or goal can act as organizer – rather than the usually siloed direction of functional leaders.
- Encourages the repurposing of information. Even the act of filing one piece of information under one "tag" places it in a silo. Using multiple tags may make it discoverable by more people to whom it matters – to whom it is relevant. Each time that happens they may find a new use – or a new way to package that information.
- Delivers lateral thinking and new perspectives. If you are working on controlling the head on a pint of beer and tag your project "foam," and you find a colleague working in the lubricants industry who has also tagged their work "foam" (a potential cause of harm in his business), there's an excellent chance your different perspectives will find value in each other's challenges. In large organizations, without the "share" you may never know each other exists.
- Prompts value exchanges which reinforce connections and relationships. In the foam case referenced above, people from very different parts of a business have found they share common goals and can bring value to each other. They have made vital new connections – and ones which tear down functional, divisional, and departmental silos.
- Cuts costs, saves time. Not only will the collaboration that Shareability delivers help you find better solutions to shared problems, faster, it'll also make sure you aren't unknowingly replicating effort due to operating in isolated pockets. At Unilever the team working on an ice cream problem in Europe didn't even know they had counterparts

in South America until one of the earliest internal social networks got built. It turned out they were both working on the same issue, according to technologist and entrepreneur Dr Chris Thorpe who was part of the NoHo Digital team which developed the platform in 1997.

• Ensures an organization learns collectively – and faster. Once our ice cream techies cracked their problem they could now share that learning across the whole of the business. Tagged effectively it would remain available to prevent wheels being reinvented ad infinitum. That means best practice gets found, built up, and shared at the right time to the right people.

• Finally – if allowed, Shareability provides the tools for a radical re-organization of resource. Deployed effectively it means people gravitate to what they care most about and can do most about. It can allocate people to work with their passions, generating a giant leap in effectiveness and productivity – not to mention morale.

An organization living Shareability would use email only sparingly – because knowledge and information is often chaotically organized in attachments, inappropriate subject lines, and "all-staffers" which end up feeling irrelevant to "all-staff." It is very hard to use search effectively with them.

Imagine trying to find who is working on what via a search across every email in the business in real time. Email doesn't deliver that. It swallows documents galore on a daily basis – never to be referenced again. Like a filing cabinet (but often with less indexing) it sucks in information. As organizations get larger and access to the "people who know" gets more and more distant, email sucks ever harder. Before long you have a full-on black hole of information swallowing everything and letting nothing out.

email ... swallows documents galore on a daily basis

Shareability aims to reverse that. The principle encourages you to choose collaborative documents – such as Google docs, on which more than one person can work at a time – from the start. The documents would be tagged in a shared space enabling effective search and retrieval of information.

Search is essential for two reasons – discovery of information and discovery of people. Finding others working on the thing you are also trying to crack is a clear bonus of aiming for Shareability.

If the organization is designed to allow groups to form in a relatively ad hoc way, then through the process of discovering who is trying to solve the same problem, and what their take on the problem is, we can move to solutions much faster. This demands a flattening of the structure or discovery gets stifled by lines of managers demanding each employee stays in the box they've been allocated – focused only on delivering against the directions their bosses have issued.

If this free-form management sounds a little utopian we should cast an eye toward the fastest-growing major company of the century so far – Google – where the "20% rule" is king.

Every member of the engineering staff has 20% of their time purposefully focused on projects of their own interest – stuff that isn't in their job description. (Note it's not 100% time, even at Google). The work conducted in that "free" time should be Google-related of course – but it is something they are more likely to be passionate about than the thing they have been otherwise directed to do.

You can bet that passion – and sharing it through the way the projects get documented and talked about internally – attracts others who share the passion to share their ideas and help reach the goal. Gmail (Google's free and premium-for-business email service) came out of 20% time. 3M has had a similar "15% time" enshrined since 1948. Among its outputs is the ubiquitous Post-it note.

Not only does this kind of thinking, by necessity, cede control to employees over managers – at least for part of their time – it also gives staff responsibility. It's really up to them what to do in that time.

* * *

At multinational Fluor, a business which executes complex engineering, procurement, construction, and maintenance projects for commercial concerns and governments around the globe, sharing what it knows among 41,000 staff at 60 global offices on six continents is core to success.

Headquartered in Irving, Texas, its people hold degrees in more than 100 engineering and 60 scientific fields. They share what they know through an award-winning knowledge management system called Knowledge Online.

Collaboration strategist Jeff Hester has played a pivotal role in designing knowledge-sharing approaches and systems at Fluor. He started out as an engineer at a competitor to Fluor. Experience in smaller companies after that first job influenced much of his thinking today.

Jeff, who is based in Los Angeles, California, learnt much from the start-up environment – which he was able to take with him into Fluor when he joined in 1988.

"One of the primary reasons they brought me in was that I had some unique skills in computer-aided design" (Jeff has co-authored books on CAD).

"Very quickly in my career I had started applying automation technology to engineering problems.

Jeff continues: "The Internet came along, but even prior to that a lot of my book projects had been helped by networking through Compuserve (America's first commercial online service) and things like that.

"So I was already involved in a collaborative environment online and understood the value of online communities and being able to connect with people. So when the Internet rolled out in the '90s, I was very interested."

He got involved in creating Fluor's initial intranet and defining the governance rules around it.

A few years later Jeff stepped outside of the security of the big enterprise to join a dot-com as employee number 16 in a software company. After three years the company hit the buffers and Jeff had to look for his next challenge. It was then, in 2001, that he was asked to return to Fluor to help on a new knowledge management tool.

"For the last 12 years I have been involved, pretty much, on that." Jeff works with a team of 10 on it but there is an extended network with distributed governance.

"Our model is built on communities of practice (we call them knowledge communities). We believe the people who own the content, the domain experts, are the people who should manage the communities. Control shouldn't be in some ivory tower.

"Within each you have a sponsor and a leader, who sets the strategic direction, a knowledge manager who does the operations and the tactical implementation of the strategy, and that's worked very well for us over the years," says Jeff.

But now Fluor is looking at taking its Shareability to the next step. Communities of practice tend to organize around functional areas (e.g., electrical engineering).

"We have global excellence leaders who define the strategic direction for their function, understand the resources available, what key knowledge and expertise we need. The community of practice is their focal point."

They are expanding this approach with a focus on the project side. Projects require the combination of many functional areas – and a much less siloed approach. In 2012 they implemented IBM's Connections (of which you can read more in our chapter on Connectedness) as an informal collaboration space. Now, says Jeff, Fluor is moving to integrate existing knowledge communities within that environment, and also creating project communities.

The process has caused a shift in Jeff's role too – toward social collaboration with a specific focus on the process of project execution. Improving how Fluor shares knowledge (and therefore how its teams work together more effectively) is regarded as a pivotal part of the corporation's global strategy as laid out by CEO and Chairman David T Seaton.

"By the year 2020 we want to double in size. In order to do that, we want to deliver projects in half the time, at half the cost.

"To do that we have to be very effective about how we leverage and re-use knowledge and expertise," says Jeff.

That means maintaining the communities of practice where expertise and best practice are built and shared, but adding communities of projects, where day-to-day problems must be solved, where collaboration across functional areas is essential.

One of the barriers, says Jeff, is that people get very focused on the task at hand. They are therefore not thinking about how what they are doing could help people on another project somewhere else or in the future.

what they are doing could help people on another project

How can Shareability be designed-in?

Currently (as of July 2013) Fluor has very large communities. Staff are opted-in and, since CVs are uploaded, the system indexes their skills and makes them discoverable through the use of simple search. It will find documents or people regardless of where the key terms are indexed in the knowledge management system, no matter which community it has been discussed in, or filed with.

Having skills and knowledge discoverable through search (rather than lost in email) is an essential for Shareability. Immediately, the silos are removed.

But search needs filters.

"We have a rigor behind the identification of experts. Each of the community leaders can identify, on a global basis, who the top-notch experts are, and we designate that, it shows up in their profile, and alongside their username in forums, for example," Jeff explains.

That means those searching, or asking questions of the community, have a shortcut to information they can rely on. There is a weighting for expertise in the search returns. Staff can filter by people/discussions/knowledge/news/links, too.

Assuming you find the expertise you need, what does Fluor do to support their collaboration with you?

"That's where some personal skills get involved. One option is to contact the person directly and ask for help," says Jeff.

But he also notes that not everyone will find someone they feel comfortable contacting, in their search returns. So the alternative is to post a question. Now the choice is with those who will or will not respond – a filter of its own.

Designated subject matter experts have a commitment to responding as readily as they are able. Sharing knowledge in the organization is also part of your performance appraisal at Fluor. At the top of the technical career track are fellows and senior fellows.

"Fellows have a budget for attending conferences, writing white papers, and pursuing new technology," says Jeff.

Fluor has avoided giving specific rewards for sharing knowledge and instead focuses on recognition – putting a personal face on the stories of success. When you log into the Fluor system you will see news, highlighting how somebody has been sharing what they know, with a success story supporting that. There is a peer-recognition award, too – called the KM Pace-setter.

"Any employee can nominate any other employee. When that happens they get a nice email to congratulate and thank them. And at the end of October each year we review all the nominations (last year we had over 1000) and we evaluate each," says Jeff.

Those that win (around 140 in 2012) get a certificate presented in a local-office ceremony. And they get a badge on their profile for the year.

"One of our senior fellows in Johannesburg, South Africa, has been in the company for 30 years. He's a top expert. He said he didn't feel like he needed to have anyone pat him on the back and tell him he was doing a good job. Even so, when he gets one of the nomination letters, he admits he smiles, it makes him feel good," says Jeff.

The toughest part of all is moving Shareability out of knowledge and expertise and into time and resource management. How can the organization enable the flexibility for individuals to shift their work focus for chunks of time to collaborate with each other rather than on their "day job"?

At Fluor, says Jeff, there is an expectation that staff will also be working on what the company describes as "Portfolio Assignments," that is, things that are not directly in their job description.

"Whether there is budget for that depends upon what the project is," admits Jeff.

"It's a tug of war. Often there is no explicit budget, or you have to make a case for budget. When you get far enough up the organization to people like the fellows and the senior fellows, those guys have time budgeted in to do things like that."

In short Fluor has built in some capacity as a default for the most expert and effective knowledge sharers. In other cases the capacity has to be fought for with a supporting business case.

Part of the design issue of Shareability for the organization is a simple thing like technical barriers. People talk plenty around a restaurant table. There is no technical barrier and much to be gleaned from incidental rather than initiated conversation.

It is unlikely that I will initiate a conversation to tell you something is just "okay" (last night's meal/movie/concert, for example). I will initiate if I thought last night's meal/movie/concert was great or terrible. I will regard this as information you need to know. But there is almost as much value in you knowing that I thought any of those experiences was just "okay." But we will only share that through incidental conversation (as and when it crops up in conversations initiated for other reasons).

Jeff is looking at ways of reducing barriers to the initiation of conversation and therefore tapping into the incidental. One example he cites is

Squiggle which, with the appropriate video support, allows small teams to see each other's status, and a webcam view (updated every few seconds) of whether they are on the phone, at their desk, etc. You simply touch the screen to initiate a video conversation with the person you see as available, and drag and drop others into the conversation if their involvement becomes relevant.

Jeff says: "The challenge is, how do we make it really easy for people to share knowledge – how do I create frictionless knowledge sharing, so there's no extra effort on the part of the guy on the project? We are looking at three ways of doing that:

"One is direct touch, which we are developing: Have a knowledge management professional who works on a project on a periodic basis and really mines that project for what is valuable for future projects.

"Another is personal participation. We also have many individuals who understand that it is valuable for both the company and for their own individual brand within the company to share their knowledge.

"The third area is automating knowledge capture and sharing to some degree. I'm not sure yet what that is going to look like. We are looking at re-use libraries and making them searchable and accessible without pre-qualifying the information. Over time we can let their use or re-use reveal how valuable the information is," Jeff adds.

It is a little like putting all your recycling into one bucket and letting someone else later decide which "useful" pile to place it in.

What all systems of this kind must guard against is that one man's trash is another man's gold. Without context there is no meaning. The crowd should do the labeling – and constant relabeling to avoid this. Miscellaneous, multi-tagged (or indexed) labeling allows value to emerge based on an individual's (or team's) context.

How does Jeff measure success? Initially engagement metrics are important, to show take up. But activity does not equal value.

"Measuring value is a much trickier thing to do. We've tried looking at the average time saved by someone downloading knowledge rather than re-creating it, but it never seems very credible.

"What we have found over time is our success stories, our anecdotes, are more real. We have an annual Success Story contest; we review those stories around November. I'll give you an example:

"We had an engineer working on a project in Kuwait. There were 16 people at that location – so he had limited resources locally. The project would ordinarily have required some very specialized equipment, but the engineer said, 'I think there may be a better way to do this.'

"He went into the Knowledge Management system and asked the question, got expert feedback from three different locations, took that back to the client and was able to eliminate a large piece of equipment.

"And that saved 750m euros," says Jeff.

If your organization is not actively on the path to Shareability yet, how can you get started?

Jeff suggests starting conversations with those people within your organization who are already using collaborative tools to share what they know. Even if they have not had IT approval, even if they are doing it on their smartphones, you can be sure your staff, at least in pockets, are already helping each other succeed.

Find out why they do that, what benefit they get from it.

Listen to them to find out how you could help them succeed, too.

* * *

Economist, blogger, and technologist JP Rangaswami – chief scientist at Salesforce and former chief scientist at BT – has an interesting way of describing the difference in organizational requirements of a company built on the principle of Shareability.

Indian by birth, JP tells how when he lived in Calcutta, if he bumped into a few friends on his way home it was always easy and natural to invite them to join his family for dinner.

In England this is much harder to do, he argues. That is because our food is structured differently: You may have four steaks ready at home to feed four people. If another three turn up, sharing becomes awkward.

Indian food is more granular, easier to redistribute. It is structured for sharing.

And it's this kind of thinking you have to embed in the structure of an Open Business, smaller, more flexible units of information – and potentially of teams.

Competition is often touted as the powerhouse of successful growth. Beat the market or sink, they say (or used to, before "too big to fail" came along …). The battleground/adversarial approach has even worked successfully within companies. Successive UK governments have tried unleashing it on the National Health Service – even on education.

There was little collaborative about the way media company Emap operated in its fastest growing years for example. The consumer publishing company (as it was at the time – and as it was when I spent 20 years of my career within it) housed several motorcycle magazines within one building. All they shared (apart from healthy contempt for each other) was a desire to beat each other. Journalists on the same titles would fight against each other to claim the glory of the best stories. If they had to share anything it was more likely to be with a foreign magazine from another company altogether.

Despite what the collaboration canon tells us, from *Harvard Business Review* to Wikinomics, it worked. Spectacularly.

For many years Emap's growth made it among the most admired companies on the FTSE. And others have either adopted the model or arrived at it independently – promoting the cut-throat over the collaborative, the "I" over the team, keeping over sharing. And they think it works.

But they kid themselves because success is relative. They may be doing a satisfactory job, but could they do so much better by adopting a more collaborative approach – aggregating and distributing best practice rather than hoarding the tricks that allow some to win as others lose?

Collaboration allows more to shine while the competitive approach results in someone in the shade for every shining light. In other words, collaboration is a better way to scale happiness. And no business succeeds when morale is shot.

collaboration is a better way to scale happiness

The no-share model may have a place: where it is vital that the various parts of your company have distinct cultures and generate distinct outputs then there is potentially risk in sharing. In our Emap example, if the bike magazines shared their exclusives, their contacts, their leads, their way of writing, their picture choices – well they would have all shared the same character. And it was the differences which attracted readers, allowing them to label themselves through the choices they made.

Where you want to deliver a consistent outcome (if you are representing different products but under the banner of the same brand, for example) collaborate internally. If you need to be different, compete internally.

But even here collaboration can help. It can help you shape the processes you can apply to reach very different and relevant outcomes. One best-practice process can result in very different outputs, providing the inputs are different.

You can take some simple steps toward Shareability by investigating the Creative Commons movement and considering what you have that it would be wise to publish outside the organization for others to share.

Creative Commons is a non-profit organization that "enables the sharing and use of creativity and knowledge through free legal tools." It does so with the ambition of providing "universal access to research and education with the intention of driving a new era of growth and productivity."

It offers alternative copyright licenses allowing you to take safe, trial steps away from the usual big business default of "all rights reserved" to "some rights reserved." You can specify that it is fine to replicate your content provided it is not for someone else to make profit from, for example. You can let individuals share your pictures, but insist that companies pay to use.

The official website of the President of the United States is published under a Creative Commons license.

Glaxo SmithKline is sharing its malarial data set (which includes more than 13,500 compounds known to be active against malaria) under another Creative Commons license. According to a case study reported on Creative Commons's own website Glaxo SmithKline has surrendered all its copyright claim to the data to place it in the public domain. A GSK statement read:

> By making this information publicly available GSK hopes that many other scientists will review this information and analyse the data faster than we could on our own ... this will help drive the discovery of new medicines. We encourage other groups, including academics and other pharmaceutical companies, to make their own compounds and related information publicly available.

Summary

Shareability is the packaging of knowledge for easy and open sharing internally and externally. It is where the organizational design principles of collaboration reside – flattening hierarchies, distributing responsibility, and making the organization more strategy and goal led than management and task directed.

GOAL STATE / WORST CASE

Where does your business stand from 1 to 5?

Goal state (*scores 5/5*)

Knowledge/thought leadership in all formats is created in such a way that it can be easily and readily published openly, and shared. Share functions are built into each document/asset. Creative Commons is the default.

Worst case (*scores 1/5*)

Knowledge created in the organization stays within the organization. Anything published outside is done so with extensive copyright protections in place.

First **steps** ...

If you estimate your organization is poor at this start by:

1. Talking to staff who already collaborate with their own tools and devices. Learn why they do this and identify how you could better support them.
2. Considering the use of Creative Commons licenses on a trial basis.
3. Recognizing and rewarding staff for sharing what they know.
4. Identifying the business benefit you want to achieve through increased Shareability (e.g., faster/lower-cost project delivery). Place a value on this.
5. Allocating a budget based on the business benefit you seek to achieve. Remember this budget must resource people/processes/technology. Resource for team flexibility.
6. Developing a plan informed by Connectedness (Chapter 5).

Connectedness

/ Definition

Connecting all employees to one another and externally through open social media.

If Shareability is the cultural key to collaboration, then, at its simplest, Connectedness is the wiring that makes it all happen. It would be easy therefore to conclude that Connectedness is a relatively simple piece of technical, tactical tool selection.

But the reality is that Shareability and Connectedness have a more organic relationship than can be simply delineated. One feeds the other, and vice versa. The more connected you are, the more you can share. The more you want to share, the more you want to connect. The inter relationship is what drives collaboration and the best Open Businesses.

If you simply give everyone a phone on their desk and select the best wiring provider, you are still a long way from effective use of the connection. And if this phone thing is all new to your team, then it is more likely to gather dust than new business.

We have seen many companies simply buying tools and discovering the technical solution is not enough. The expression: "All The Gear But No Idea" springs to mind. It is the position so many organizations find themselves in having been sold on the tech – convinced by slick sales folk that there really is a button you can click to make you "social." Next they will be telling us there is one that generates insight, too ...

Sure, you need the gear. But first, get the idea. I guarantee you'll make better selections of the gear as a result.

So the fifth Principle of Open Business is Connectedness: not simply a matter of buying the right software.

This is really worth spelling out because many harassed executives fall for the approach. They know they must start making their business operate in a more connected way internally. They know closer connections to customers are important, too. What they don't know is how to achieve this. Along comes a tech vendor who offers a magic bullet and our harassed executive can tick his "social platform" box, tell the board he has it covered, and carry on: Business As Usual.

It is essential to understand that Connectedness is part of organizational design – not simply a physical fact of connecting *A* to *B*. Without the attending cultural shift required, our harassed executive will have landed themselves with yet another layer of technology for the IT department to ring-fence and control – and no new value created.

Once again, we invite you to score your organization against this principle and offer a guide at the end of this chapter to help you do so.

True, there is only so far along the road to Open that you can travel without a digital way to connect within the organization and without. But the decision on which way to do this should be a secondary consideration. Achieving the cultural shift to be an organization which values Connectedness comes first. Opening the flow of dialogue often has to start

the cultural shift ... comes first

inside but it must always reach beyond the boundaries of the organization to scale the value available when we connect.

The alternative end of that scale is a world in which no one is allowed to use the web to find solutions. We're at the point now that companies which restrict Connectedness do so to their own cost. So many staff have smartphones now, they will find a way around bans in any event. Indeed, analysts Gartner are now predicting 70% of mobile professionals will conduct their work on personal devices by 2018.

I have seen companies that don't even allow access to Google during office hours (a little like saying we would rather pretend the world doesn't exist). Today there are still companies restricting access to social media sites – yet these are often the richest flows of information on which anyone in the organization should be basing real-time decisions. A strong case can be made that senior executives who are *not* connected should be regarded as being derelict in their duty.

Senior executives must be close to their staff and their staff's needs, their customers and their customers' needs, they must have their fingers on the pulse of their industry, of emerging thinking, of key people to know, of potentially disruptive innovations, of new entrants, of tides of relevant public opinion. These are the essential need-to-knows for business leaders. All of these are delivered at low cost, with high speed and relevance by being connected. All must be mediated, therefore more slowly and more opaquely delivered when you are not.

"Oh, but no one talks about my industry in social media," I hear the last of the Luddites mumble. Wrong. Go take a look. I haven't seen an industry yet where this is true.

"Oh, but I don't have time for all this." Wrong. Effective use of social platforms will speed up the delivery of relevance to your inbox. You can do most of it on your smartphone, from the back of your taxi, your seat on the train and, with increasing regularity, from the cabin of your plane.

"Oh, but I leave this sort of thing to the kids and the interns." Wrong. You are handing direct relationships with key stakeholders (such as staff and customers) to those with least experience and least to lose.

"Oh, but this new technology stuff is too hard to learn for me now …" Wrong. Social platforms are incredibly user friendly. That's why so many people have learned to use them without a manual.

Go and try. You are derelict in your duties to your shareholders, your team, your customers, and yourself if you do not.

Rather than work against Connectedness (usually out of fear), work with it. You will be working in the same direction as your teams.

Without our daily connections to others, our ideas remain un-nurtured and un-tested, our understanding of the realities of the ecosystem within which we all live, severely limited. This ecosystem, this market, is not something you can take a snapshot of once a year. It is ever changing, something you are part of and which must be listened and responded to, in as close to real time as possible, if you are to maintain a best possible fit with its needs.

Connectedness is an essential part of this. Connectedness scales the organization's ability to listen, respond, and adapt to the market. Connectedness provides an early warning system for changing need, for rising dissatis- faction, for new competitors.

an early warning system for changing need

But beyond all of this, Connectedness humanizes a business. It allows your customers and other stakeholders to interact with the living, breathing, passionate, caring people on whom your business depends. It takes down the walls both internally and externally. Using the digital tools at our disposal enables humanization at scale. Simply – your people can talk to people. Other people like this. Your people like this. You should like this. You should do this – personally.

The fear may be that some will abuse the freedom. That they will waste all day fraternizing on Facebook or taking time out on Twitter or on your own internal social networks. But the fact is, that is a management issue, not a technology one – or even a cultural one. Don't blame social media if you've selected the wrong employees or have failed to manage them effectively.

Great employees, the ones you want on your team, know the value of building relationships (internally and externally) to achieve shared aims. If you've got your (Principle 1) Purpose right, your staff will be exactly the kind who do what they do all day every day in pursuit of the goals they share with your organization. Give them tools to do this more effectively and they will deliver with honesty and integrity.

It comes down to another of the key principles we will discuss later – Trust. If you trust your employees enough to put them in a uniform and place them in front of customers, or if you trust them enough to pay them for the tasks they perform, then trust them enough to connect with each other internally and externally, on your behalf.

Of course, you may want to create some governance to protect yourself initially – training, guidelines, protocols. But do so with the understanding that these are simply signposts of the cultural change you are aiming to achieve – that they are a step on the road to Open.

Among the most powerful benefits Connectedness will deliver, are that it:

- Provides networks for information sharing and collaboration
- Demonstrates openness and accountability – improving customer satisfaction
- Increases the opportunity for serendipity and innovation – inside and out of the organization
- Humanizes your company – making business personal in the way most humans crave
- Allows employees to grow, build, and manage relationships with customers and partners more effectively – improving retention
- Connects organizations to their employees' personal networks which can scale collective reach
- Enables two-way flows of information and intelligence, improving market knowledge in real time

Global luxury brand Burberry has committed to being the first "digital end-to-end" company. The former CEO Angela Ahrendts says: "You have to be totally connected with everyone who touches your brand. If you're not I don't know what your business model is going to be in five years." Burberry's social strategies have been credited with a 10% rise in same-store sales (source: beingpeterkim.com).

Internal social tool Yammer (best described as Twitter for the enterprise) has been deployed to connect employees in 200,000 companies worldwide (including the likes of DHL, Cap Gemini, Shell, and 7-Eleven). A Forrester report on the total economic impact of deploying such a social tool over a three-year period in a company of 21,000 employees with one-third using the tool, measured: "a risk-adjusted return on investment of 365 per cent with a payback period of 4.3 months and $5.7 million in net present value" (source: Forrester Research).

Connectedness is an open communication methodology which must play out throughout the entirety of the organization. Without such a coherent approach, businesses will start to suffer negative economies of scale when it comes to their distributed workforces.

Connecting your people creates value, which is something Carol Sormilic is deeply familiar with. Carol has been an IBM employee for over 30 years, rising to the role of vice president and transformation executive for IBM's Global Workforce and Web Processes. Home is currently Connecticut. But she has lived through a series of cycles in the business, which have taken her to Europe and Asia and given her a unique global insight on the needs and benefits of Connectedness.

She worked on the first personal computers (buying the microprocessors for them), became an executive at IBM during the preparation for Y2K (working to co-ordinate IBM's global preparations for the potential risks surrounding the date change from 1999 to 2000). What she learned in managing that huge global project was called on again when she was asked to lead the internal transition of all systems for the euro currency. She spent two-and-a-half years in Paris leading that. Returning to the US she picked up on her earlier interest in IBM's intranet – and looking at what processes and applications could sensibly be moved to it.

"I have a history of looking at how we do things and figuring out how to streamline, simplify, and free-up people's time to focus on higher value-add activities," says Carol.

In the last two years her focus has been on helping to change the way IBM works internally. "My role today is looking at various techniques and technologies to put information and expertise at the fingertips of our employees," she adds.

Part of this has been about creating a collaboration framework.

"What we found was that there were specific pockets, groups of people who were all using their own methods (and tools) for collaborating," says Carol.

The problem was that they were creating their own silos. If two pockets didn't use the same tools or techniques then they couldn't collaborate with each other. The answer lay in good project-planning: setting goal states, auditing current activities and tools, assessing the gaps, and acting to fill them.

"We asked ourselves how we could create an enterprise collaboration framework – and then how do we select the best tools for the various aspects of collaboration, and get everybody using the same tools, so that you could share across borders, across silos, etc.," says Carol.

With that – and a healthy dose of IBM innovation – they created an internal social collaboration platform.

In 2010 Carol went to China challenged with testing her vision for an open and connected workplace of the future in a very new environment.

"It was really my two years there that pushed me to believe even more strongly in working in an Open environment and with social tools," she says. Now that Carol has helped the business formalize how people can connect in IBM, is she seeing a Cambrian explosion of emerging value from the connections being made?

"If I look at the amount of content being shared, the size of people's networks, the numbers of downloads and re-use of material, the indicators that people are collaborating are really quite extensive," she says.

The connections don't end at the edge of the company. Through ibm.com customers and other interested parties can join in conversations and share knowledge with people inside the company. In fact the external platform came first (in 2008) with the internal following a year later.

The social platform used internally is the same sold to customers, called, appropriately enough, IBM Connections. IBM Sametime is another element of the suite; the latest in a long history of real-time (synchronous) communication tools.

"When we went to instant messaging in 1999," says Carol, "it was a big change for the company. It really flattened our company and got rid of hierarchy. People learned that they could reach out to anybody in the organization, connect with them, and get answers very quickly. It really became the foundation of people being less concerned about who they were contacting (in terms of 'rank') because the primary thing became how quickly they could get the help they needed. Today IBMers send 50 million instant messages a day. It shows the rate at which connection is happening."

Carol is evidence of the flattened hierarchy herself. She is a VP who will happily respond to messages from people of whatever level – even in her kitchen in the evenings.

"I'll have numerous teammates who may be from India, may be new to the team, may be working on a project I'm associated with. They see that I am online and they reach out and ask me a question. They aren't concerned with levels or status within the company, they just hope that I'm going to know the answer – and if I don't that I can point them in the right direction. We live and breathe it every day," she says.

Carol says what Connectedness has done is made people feel entitled and empowered to seek the best, fastest solutions to their problems – no matter where that takes them in the organization.

empowered to seek the best, fastest solutions

For some senior executives the idea of staff contacting them at home for a quick steer is the stuff of nightmares. Others will be concerned that some people in the organization could rapidly become very well known for their expertise and end up over-loaded with calls for help as a result. In short, how does IBM ameliorate the risk of too much traffic going through too few individuals?

"If you have one key expert on a particular topic and they are the only person that people are going to, that person has ways of managing access to them. They can put up a Do Not Disturb on their instant messaging, or they can say they are in a meeting.

"You can completely disconnect, but what is interesting is that most people don't do that. They choose instead to make clear what their current choice is and others seem to be very respectful of that."

IBM also has tools which allow staff to elect to share what they are expert in and also when and how they would like to be contacted, and how much time they are able to give. IBM found people had already started using their own tools to collaborate before standard ones (and processes) were introduced. They had already started to create a culture of Connectedness. In many ways the tools were supporting what people were already doing, wanted to do, and saw value in doing.

Where had the imperative come from? IBM's moment of need came in the shift of perspective required to become a globally integrated enterprise. What that meant was IBM no longer had "floor-to-ceiling" businesses in each country; each with their own HR, Finance, Integrated Supply Chain, Customer Fulfillment, Sales and Distribution departments, etc. Instead IBM looked at a horizontal approach of having end-to-end processes.

"Instead of a series of sister teams around the world doing similar work, IBM flattened the organization, having an end-to-end horizontal process and then having the people associated with those processes working on the same team," says Carol.

"We'd been successful with the adoption of instant messaging, but then when we got to integrating the global enterprise the big questions became 'What do you do about time zones? What do you do about cultural differences? Language differences? What about trying to help find leaders who may be in different parts of the world? How do you make sure that content gets re-used rather than every team recreating the same types of material?'

"We had to figure out how these teams could connect to each other and to content," says Carol.

The way IBM worked had changed, creating a massive new and urgent need to connect. That started with defining a process for collaboration, followed by an inventory of all the tools in current use, and the definition of various need states for collaboration:

- I need to find information or expertise to help me do this job;
- I need to get to know that information and know that expertise;
- I need to work together (to create content, to share content, do research together, etc.);
- I need to recognize or recommend expertise.

Then IBM went about identifying the best tools which could become their enterprise solution. Where there were gaps the IBM Innovation team started building solutions.

"We have a place where early adopters can go and innovate. The CIO (chief information officer) provides a Technology Adoption Program, also called TAP. People can go in, get space, innovate. They get the crowd to rate their innovation and then we look at how we can harvest that into products or into production," says Carol.

And it is from this research and innovation that their own platform for connection emerged. One of the secrets of IBM's success was the way the tool set was introduced.

"IBM didn't say 'Here are all the tools that the CIO says you need to use.' We picked methodologies and tools that other parts of the business were using so the matrix of recommended tools and methodologies represented best practices from different areas of the business. We may have chosen one best practice from our software group, another from our consulting group … so people could see that something they had worked on was selected as a best practice and that really helped with buy-in," says Carol.

It was the collective knowledge of the enterprise that made the recommendations for the enterprise.

"When people put a lot of time and effort into doing something for their team and they are then told to use somebody else's tool or method it's much harder to get that buy-in," Carol warns.

Apart from the open collaboration happening through the connections any "outsider" can make at ibm.com, there are huge numbers of "IBMers" active outside of IBM in social media in both personal and professional capacities. Twitter, Facebook, and LinkedIn appear to be particular favorites. When there was an uplift in people using social media and working inside/outside the firewall – working socially as Carol puts it – a group of interested IBMers came together to establish ground rules for themselves – much as happened at the BBC when BBC bloggers defined their own set of rules.

Carol says: "The crowd iterated on their original guidelines, self-directed, and built on as new things were learned and new spaces were opened. Clients started asking about how we guided our employees, so we published those guidelines online so any one could reference them."

More recently they have added to this a project called The Digital IBMer.

Sitting on the IBM intranet, it is a place staff can go to learn about building their digital "eminence." They can learn the basics of Twitter, Facebook, LinkedIn. They can learn how to behave in social spaces, how to help their peers, effective uses of social media for learning, effective ways to connect teams, and effective ways of using social to keep globally distributed teams together – even how to keep themselves and their families safe online. All employees are required to go through the Digital IBMer program – with a very significant take up.

IBM has clearly made Connectedness a priority. It has invested and believed in it. Given the global integration phase of its life it is easy to argue Connectedness has been an absolute essential.

We've already seen how it has resulted in new software platforms and solutions which are now commercial products available externally.

What other benefits has it delivered?

The Generation-Open project (Gen-O) has targeted boosting collaboration in common projects among those writing, maintaining, and developing code for internal projects. It offers a score card to reward and recognize how much people are contributing; how much code they are writing, how much they re-use code (that scores participants even more points), and how much they work together.

"We saw at least a 30% reduction in cycle time for getting projects done. There were significant benefits in the quality of code. There were experts in the same communities who were able to guide more junior members," says Carol. That accelerated improvements in quality and personnel development.

"Having information, or code, cataloged so you could re-use instead of re-create made the amount of re-use incredible," she adds.

Some of IBM's measures for success now include the amount of material being re-used and downloaded and shared. Every re-use and re-discovery is a significant saving in both time and cost.

And in "Career Builder" there's a wealth of content connections awaiting those seeking to develop their skills – offering savings to the HR and Training departments.

"The bigger KPIs for me are how connected we are – measured by the effectiveness of somebody's network, how quickly we can get a message out," says Carol.

"If we look at most corporations and see how many people read their corporate news, it's a very small percentage. When Ginni Rometty (chair, president and CEO of IBM) took up her post (announced in October 2011) on her first day she did a video blog and over 50% of our population saw it in the first 72 hours (more saw it in the days to follow)."

There is power in being able to reach most of your employees in your first day at work – sharing with them what your strategies are, what you are driving the business to do.

Ginni then formed an open community. She had hundreds of responses to the video – with important thoughts about things IBM could do to help realize her strategy.

Carol's own organizational community has more than 800 contributors. Around a quarter don't even report into her function.

She uses it to document what she has discussed in meetings. That means the moment she pushes the button to post everyone knows what she has been working on and making decisions about, and what the action items are.

"Instead of me having to wait a week to get someone in my calendar so we can talk about it, as soon as the meeting is over they have a flavor of what is happening," Carol adds.

Connectedness creates a more positive culture, happier individuals, and individuals who find more meaning in their work.

"If someone sends me a note that says they want to thank members of my team for their help, then that goes in a place I've created in my social spaces called 'accolades'.

"What happens is that people in the organization see that and then the person getting the accolade gets all these virtual pats on the back," says Carol.

This is important in an organization in which 50% of the 450,000 IBM population, spread across 170 countries, do not work in traditional offices. When you can't go to the water cooler, the global team is there to congratulate and support you virtually. 50% of the staff have been in IBM less than five years. Tying this organization together is a challenge. It's one that's being solved not by command and control but by connect and enable.

the global team is there to congratulate and support you

There was a push from above to make it happen. But also, Carol points out, around one-third of the company was already engaged in forms of collaboration before it was formalized. So there was the push from below.

"Then the question was how do we get the rest of the company to do it? And that's how we get to things like The Digital IBMer," says Carol.

"When Ginni became our CEO she embraced this from day one. Not only does she embrace this, she expects it – she expects that we work this way, that we are all working Open and embracing these capabilities."

It's always helpful when you have a top-down approach as well as bottom-up.

Based on IBM's experience as a large, complex, multinational organization implementing Connectedness at scale – what tips does Carol have to offer others facing the journey they must make?

"Look at how you work today. What are the work practices and how connected is your workforce? Can they easily find expertise; can they easily find and re-use content?

"If the answer is 'no', then start to think about what tools are being used. Is the CIO offering a single platform, no matter what that platform is? Without that it's going to be really hard to mine the collective intelligence of your organization."

Start small. Start with some guidelines for use of social media, for processes of collaboration. Do things as simple as asking leaders, instead of sending newsletters to your team, to do blogs instead – revealing their focus and inviting contribution. One big lesson IBM learned is that simply adding new ways to connect won't break people of the habits they are in. You have to take away the tools they were using at the same time as providing the new, consistent ones.

"If you just add they will see it as just one more thing to do and they won't see the value in it," says Carol. "You really have to embrace the opportunity of having this collective intelligence available to all in the company. This isn't just social or fun, it's really about opening up the company (even within your own firewalls) and giving people access to each other and to information.

"And that really means you get better at delivering the right information and the right expertise to your clients – and much faster.

"I believe that companies that embrace Open work patterns will see a competitive advantage over traditional workplaces."

Summary

Connectedness is the process and tool which enable people within the organization to find the information (and people) they need as swiftly as possible. It enables the collective intelligence of the organization and, when aligned with Shareability, delivers collaboration.

GOAL STATE / WORST CASE

Where does your business stand from 1 to 5?

Goal state (*scores 5/5*)

All employees are using open social media daily for external connection and applying it to make best use of the synchronous/ asynchrynous opportunities of the global web. Internal/external comms are rarely distinguished.

Worst case (*scores 1/5*)

Social media is actively discouraged during working hours. Internal comms are one-way broadcasts from the center and kept strictly internal.

First **steps** …

If you estimate your organization is poor at this start by asking:

1. Setting an example. Are you connected to the people and information you need to be through social media? Pick the tools that suit you best and get to work.

2. Conduct an audit of the collaboration tools and processes currently in use in the organization.

3. Make an evidence and peer-informed decision on best practice for both to create a social platform for collaboration that suits the needs of your business.

4. Deploy the platform as a replacement for, not an addition to, current activity.

6

Open Innovation

Definition

Innovating with partners by sharing risk and reward in the development of products, services, and marketing.

Our sixth Principle of Open Business is Open Innovation.

To borrow the definition of founding father of the term Open Innovation, Dr Henry Chesbrough, it is:

> The use of purposive inflows and outflows of knowledge to accelerate internal innovation, and expand the markets for external use of innovation, respectively.

Once again, we invite you to score your organization against this Principle and offer a guide at the end of this chapter to help you do so.

Open Innovation and its methodology have been with us since the 1950s. Most large companies with the resources to do so have been actively looking outside their organization to other companies or institutions – such as universities – for many years and in quite structured processes.

However the integration of consumers and customers into the innovation process is often ad hoc and, even more often, applied on a superficial basis.

When done badly it becomes derided as "crowd-washing" – rarely moving beyond the focus group or marketing campaigns – driven by a desire to give the *appearance* of being engaged with customers rather than to innovate best-fit solutions with them.

The advent of social technologies lowers the barrier for companies to discover and connect with people, not just other institutions. And they can do so in real time and at scale anywhere in the world at low cost. This presents a revolutionary opportunity to integrate customers and the data they create through their online interactions, directly and/or indirectly into the innovation process to inspire, qualify, and refine.

The output is not just more innovations and more effective innovations but also a greater sense of ownership from current and future customers, and therefore – an essential in a world where trust is becoming the most valuable of currencies – greater advocacy.

The more of this you get right, the less dependent you become on interruptive, expensive and inefficient marketing – markets are built into the process of innovation not just consumption. You switch from treating people as passive consumers to thinking of them as actively involved.

The fastest growing and most innovative companies of recent decades – such as Apple, Facebook, and Google – all show that applying the principle of Open Innovation goes beyond one-off tactics. It must be in the DNA of the organization.

The organization must be designed as a platform for collaboration and innovation. Being built to innovate with and for those outside the organization is what has made these benchmarks great – Apple's App Store, Facebook's open API (application program interface), and Google's Adsense and Adwords all allow others to make the best fit – to serve the long, long tail that they could never have hoped to do alone – and in so doing surface and serve millions more effectively.

Open Innovation can't be a bolt-on – that way lays the fail of crowd-washing (marketers creating the illusion of listening through Facebook polls and such like while the usual innovation processes carry on regardless).

We believe the whole organization should be seen as a platform that uses its unique expertise to collaborate with markets to realize new innovations through processes of Open Innovation such as co-creation and crowd-sourcing. (Co-creation being the process of making with groups of stakeholders, while crowd-sourcing focuses more on scaling your access to individuals who may have approaches and therefore solutions you hadn't thought of.)

Most larger companies have experimented with the increasing number of open innovation platforms such as eYeka or consultancies such as IDEO, Face Group, or InSites, which offer virtual, real-world, or hybrid workshops and forms of structured Open Innovation to serve one or other part of the innovation process.

Few have managed to patch these constituent parts together to become a total system built to sustain ecosystems of partnerships that can consistently deliver innovations that both spin-off and spin-into their parent organizations.

Why? The sheer scale of change management required, political barriers to overcome, as well as the many moving parts of data collection, processing, partner recruitment, and management make comprehensive change an unnerving prospect.

So what we currently see are two extremes: with incumbents there is a gradual opening of innovation processes through pockets of open innovation, while new entrants are built on the Principle of Open Innovation by default – disrupting every market they touch.

One great barrier, especially for "old world" closed business, in using Open Innovation is fear of loss of control and the protectionism around ownership of IP. This is not something that has been fully resolved other than in the "open source" technology movement which is a key part of the Open Business Principle of Shareability and of Open Data, but is giving birth to interesting thinking around Co-IP in which co-innovators are rewarded with part ownership (and therefore risk and reward) depending on the level and success of their involvement – scaling through particular stages. This requires well-defined legal systems to be in place but will become critical as the competition for the most creative consumers becomes hotter.

In short this is about sharing in the risk and reward with those engaged in the process – inside or outside of the organization.

Currently this is achieved only in part by most corporations. There are some examples of companies which actually give consumers shares in the profits from their product idea.

But even this only serves to reward one ideator. It's therefore a model better suited to crowd-sourcing (rewarding the best individual idea from many offered). Co-creation is a much more collaborative approach involving multiple individuals working in concert. There may be different stakeholders at different stages. Some may only participate in one stage and drop-out at others, they may lack the time, ability, expertise, or access to contribute evenly throughout the process. Some may stay the course of the whole process.

In any event, it is not so simple to reward as there is no clear "big idea" generator. In co-creation the IP is really shared by many. Simply asking people to sign over everything they generate is neither reasonable nor likely to attract the people who can most help you.

What is therefore required is a legal/commercial principle that clearly rewards participants against the specific detail of their contribution. It should guide the level of access they get to the project, too – based on how much they want to contribute. It is conceivable that this can be decided democratically with the distribution of reward being awarded by the community involved in it.

One thing is certain; the search for the best and most relevant ideators and contributors in your industry will get increasingly harder as more and more companies identify the opportunity the process affords. If you are competing for time and energy then you need to provide incentives.

Fig 1 (devised by Jamie Burke and Steffen Hück during their time at 90:10 Group) illustrates how a Co-IP (or co-patent) model could work alongside the Creative Commons movement (for shared attribution).

Change must come because trying innovation behind closed doors and occasionally sense-checking with focus groups can no longer keep pace with those organizations which are fully networked and open to market collaboration, nor can it deliver the same level of transformational innovation.

Open Innovation is not about handing over your company to the crowd but partnering with its selected representatives in a structured way that combines their needs, ideas, and opinions with your team's professional wisdom and IP.

Get it right and you:

• Distribute the risk of innovating among those getting the rewards
• Reduce the risk that the innovations won't fit the needs of the intended market
• Develop customer ownership of the innovation pre-launch
• Allow external ideas to be surfaced early in the process
• Scale effective idea generation and development

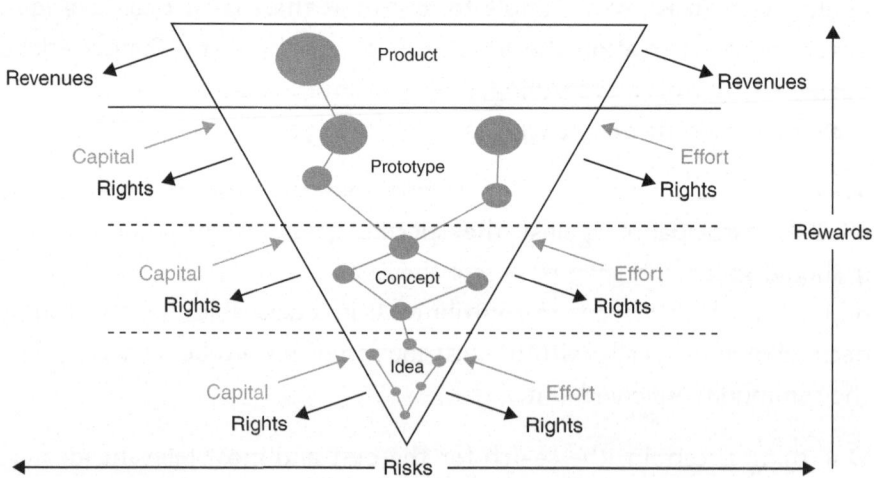

FIG 1   Co-IP: Sharing risk, reward, effort, and rights. Illustration by Jamie Burke and Steffen Hück.

Can you put a value on it? When multinational agribusiness Syngenta adopted Open Innovation processes, Forrester compared the total economic impact compared to traditional closed methods of innovation. They saw an ROI of 182% with payback in less than two months. In addition to financial returns, the study revealed qualitative benefits including greater efficiencies, cost savings, and productivity. (Source: Forrester Consulting, "The Total Economic Impact of InnoCentive's Enterprise Solution," April 2010).

Through the Open Basque project in Spain, Luis Berasategi and Eduardo Castellano have been seeking to identify a set of guidelines and processes for the effective deployment of Open Innovation across the region. They work with the support of Mondragon – a co-operative which posts revenues in the region of $20bn a year and which employs around 100,000 people.

It's Spain's fourth biggest company. Innovation is Mondragon's life blood. It files an invention patent every week.

Their model – developed at not-for-profit research organization IK4-Ikerlan – is currently being tested with one of the group's largest supermarket chains, Eroski. It has been used to trial co-creation with customers – with a focus on the fish trade. At time of writing the researchers were awaiting results. They have fostered a community to help define the company's offerings: for example, the kind of product it sells, its services, and channels. Test and learn will be conducted in one store to be rolled out across the rest of the group's outlets.

The model was arrived at through working with a wide and representative set of Mondragon companies.

In brief, the model – first published in January 2013 – suggests to get started you should follow these three phases:

1. Initiation

   Define draft objectives
   Define core-group members
   Define how long you will incubate the project for

2. Design

> Identify necessary competencies
> Indentify stakeholder roles (inventor, transformer, financier, connector)
> Define collaboration strategy
> Identify source of funding

3. Creation/Set up

> Establish mission/business model
> Establish collaboration process
> Shape contract and agreements
> Establish legal and financial structure
> Define how governance will be applied

The researchers say these should not be seen as a set of rules, but as guidelines, and suggest anyone who wants to take their first steps into Open Innovation should first diagnose what they already have by way of active innovation processes going on in the business.

diagnose what [you] already have by way of active innovation processes

"What is the minimum we can do to test? First identify what you want to do, then identify the practices you are already doing. Maybe they can help? Then, let's see what is missing and fill the gap," said Eduardo.

Some have made Open Innovation core to how they operate. It's hard to imagine the brand we will discuss next without it …

* * *

The mobile network giffgaff is one of Britain's fastest growing. Edgy new offices in Uxbridge, Greater London, are just one testament to this. The network also happens to be a business which has adopted the principles of Open Business more whole-heartedly than most. We don't think that's a coincidence.

It's driven by a clear Purpose – a wrong about its industry it strives to put right.

It is a Networked Organization – in that its customers are its direct sales and marketing department and also (and impressively) its customer service department.

It has grown through following the principle of Shareability – its business being built for peer-to-peer recommendation and distribution.

It's Member-Led to a huge degree. So much so that no one is allowed to use the word "customer" in meetings – it's always "member."

Many decisions are transparently made – and the team is striving to become ever more Transparent.

But perhaps the Principle it is the greatest exemplar of is Open Innovation.

Many will have heard of Dell's IdeaStorm – often held up to be *the* exemplar of co-creation with customers. But giffgaff CEO Mike Fairman is delighted to be able to boast the ideas generated with his community make Dell's efforts pale by comparison.

To make Open Innovation work you have to trust your customers – or in giffgaff's case, your members – which is where the giffgaff story begins.

In 2005, O2 was the biggest brand in the UK mobile market. But it knew that to keep growing it would need to look for spin-off and adjacent businesses. The first of these was broadband. Others have followed – including financial services. To create these spin-offs it had set up a New Business Division responsible for thinking up what to do next.

A member of that team had the idea that eventually led to giffgaff. That team member was Gav Thompson, he is now director of marketing innovation at O2, and he is usually credited as being the founder of giffgaff.

Gav had scribbled his idea on the back of a sheet of a paper (where all good ideas seem to start) on a flight back from the US.

Mike takes up the story: "He had been at a Web 2.0 conference in the States – by all accounts a boring one – but it was at a time when President

Obama had just been elected for his first term through social media, Wikipedia was on the up, etc., etc.

"So he asked, 'Why can't you have a mobile business which is based around the same sort of ideas?'"

Existing mobile businesses didn't work collaboratively with their customers.

"If you look at Trust, Net Promoter Score measures, CSI (Customer Satisfaction Index) measures, stuff like that, mobile operators are ranked slightly worse than estate agents," explained Mike.

That lack of trust had been built up over time – by behaviors around contracts, around complex tariffs, price increases, keeping people on expensive legacy tariffs, etc., he added.

"In terms of the way they have acted in the past and treated their customers, they have been pretty poor," said Mike.

"All of this had been going on for years, therefore the level of trust was very low."

Gav Thompson's dream was for a mobile network run on the principle of mutuality with its members, one which rewarded its community for doing much of the work normally done by employees. He felt there was a space there for those who like to get involved and who wanted a new and different way of doing things.

And doing things in a new and different way could be the way to rebuild the trust.

And, as we consistently see, trust can only be built in an open environment. That took giffgaff on the route of needing to have conversations with its customers out loud.

"Also building trust through one-to-one conversations is not scalable, so you have to have an environment where your members can interact with each other to build the trust for themselves," said Mike. We'll return to that challenge in Chapter 10, where we look at where the Zero Moment of Truth now resides.

"Gav came up with this concept. The board looked at it and thought it was quite far out and it looks quite difficult to do from within but they thought it was a good idea and that in the UK market there would be space for it.

"Also there was a market trend in mobile where the big traditional brands were being joined by MVNO brands (mobile virtual network operators) such as Virgin, Tesco, etc. Over time they were eating into the overall market."

O2 (owned by Spain's Telefonica) wanted to be represented in the MVNO space to take advantage of that growth.

At first they considered making the offering a sub-brand of O2 but the board decided it was too different. Instead it was decided to set up giffgaff as its own business with "The Mobile Network Run by You" as its strapline. The name was taken from Scottish-English meaning "mutual giving."

"They were very good at fostering intrapreneurship," said Mike. "They said, right, we're going to treat it like a start-up business. So they said to me – 'Go set it up, you can't nick too many of our people, you can't use (apart from a tiny amount) our IT roadmap, team, or resources.' We had to go and build it ourselves."

The start-up giffgaff would have its own offices, own staff, and own governance structure.

"We have a chairman who is my day-to-day boss and we have steering committee meetings with O2 once a quarter," said Mike. It is a wholly owned subsidiary run as an independent separate limited company in the UK.

Where giffgaff can't justify having its own resource, it does share – "We don't have our own lawyers or HR," said Mike.

"The thing that attracted me was that I'd done two things already in O2 which were new, being done for the first time. I'd run the online channel, taking that from being very small to being very big. The second was starting the broadband business, getting that going and facing all the challenges of getting a mobile company to think outside of just selling mobile.

"I was only 18 months into running that and was engaged in an interesting debate with the internal communications team about forums. When we launched the broadband business I had set up a forum and we found very quickly that it was a fantastically brilliant way of actually listening to your customers," said Mike.

Quite often the team would find themselves picking up ideas direct from those forums.

"You would also pick-up 'outages' – sometimes faster than our internal systems would," said Mike.

His response – very natural in his view – was that the team should be interacting with its customers through this forum – fostering conversations between them and talking to them more.

This simple idea provoked a six-month-long debate with the internal communications team. Their view was that any staff going on to the forum to make a post were creating the equivalent of a company-sanctioned press release – and should be treated as such and therefore controlled and contained in a similar way.

"They wanted to control every single word that went on there."

Mike saw an opportunity to do more with the community, to drive more collaboration with giffgaff than O2 was allowing him with the broadband business.

"It was all about community – all about working with customers."

Mike heard about Gav's idea early on – and was full of praise for it – particularly because of the issues he'd been having in trying to create real value with forums in his part of the business. He made clear his interest to both Gav and to Gav's boss. But it took another three months of board approvals before Mike got the call that invited him to make giffgaff happen.

"When you're working in a big corporate, the opportunity to go off and set up something from scratch is brilliant. You very rarely get the opportunity to create something brand new. That was very exciting as well," said Mike.

Building a new culture was one of the challenges. Part of the giffgaff job is to be different, to be a challenger, to be unlike the big buys. If all Mike had done was recruit from the mobile industry he'd have risked creating a cookie-cutter copy.

"Probably about a third of the people were from O2, less than a third were from other mobile operators, and then the rest – about half were from very different backgrounds."

One of the first priorities was to get out of the main corporate offices as soon as possible.

"Up until October 2012 we were in a tiny little 16th-century timber-framed building in Beaconsfield" (a Buckinghamshire market town).

"We chose it deliberately to make us think differently," said Mike. He's trying to keep that difference alive in the new offices.

"It's a pretty informal place, with creative spaces. And being open plan helps a lot with working with each other. One of the things that we are working on is how we get our members more involved physically in this office – to bring them in more often," said Mike.

Idea creation is an important part – but just one part of the role of the community in giffgaff.

"One of our founding principles is that we work with our members. We call them members – not customers."

To remind everyone of this important difference there is a "honk-honk"-style horn on the table Mike and I are sat around. Every time someone uses the word customer the horn is sounded. There is one in every other meeting room, too.

"They are just little reminders. They don't get used very much but they are reminders. 'Members' and 'customers' are very different.

"Customers buy stuff from you, members do stuff with you," said Mike.

In this context an online community was essential for giffgaff to succeed.

"In fact we thought it was so essential we decided to launch it before we had our product. The launch process started with a very basic website. We said 'we are going to do mobile differently, if you're interested, sign up and we'll keep you up to date'."

That message was seeded out to a few other relevant communities and through that giffgaff was able to get a pre-launch community live and active.

"The result was that when we actually launched our mobile service, interested individuals from the community were there at midnight watching the site launch. They stayed up most of the night reading T&Cs and, by 5 a.m., they were there, very competently, answering questions from other members about those T&Cs. It was just amazing," said Mike.

It's not easy – warns Mike. Most forums fail. "There's nothing worse than finding digital tumbleweed. You're not going to ask a question if you have no chance of getting an answer."

And Q&A – particularly as customer service support – was an important part of the giffgaff business plan.

"There were three things we hoped the community would do. The first was to answer queries from other members. The second – they would help grow the business by prospecting and recommending and passing on our SIM cards, things like that," said Mike.

Anyone who signs up for giffgaff is offered a range of ways to benefit from recommending the service to others, pretty much from the word go.

"If you do recruit for us, you get rewarded through a points system," said Mike.

The third strand to the community strategy was an ideas forum. And here's where Open Innovation got its turbo boost.

The Q&A element has been very successful. There are millions of threads on the forum, the numbers of pages indexed on Google (leading searching customers to giffgaff) is in the tens of millions. The average response time to a query is about 90 seconds.

"The first answer might not be right. Each question asked gets five or six answers, but you can guarantee one of the answers will be the correct one. There's a fairly strong self-regulating system in there. If someone writes something that is rubbish another community member will be fast to put them right.

"The amazing thing is there are almost an infinite number of questions that can be asked about handsets and operating systems, our service, whatever. You can't train all of that into a customer service agent. It's impossible. So you have to have all sorts of expensive knowledge-base systems and routing around a call center, just to be able to manage that.

"The thing about community is that although none of your members knows the answer to everything, one of them *will* know the answer to any given question," Mike enthused.

He acknowledges there are limits. The community can't deal with your personal transactional data. It can't deal with billing issues. For that a small team is employed in a contact center. It's online only and it is out sourced but it is giffgaff's own team.

"It is online only," Mike emphasized. "We have never had a single customer service phone call – which I don't think any other mobile operator can say."

And if a member goes direct to the customer service team with an inquiry the community could answer for them, they get redirected back.

"The agents will say 'we recommend you go and ask the community for that'."

Over time giffgaff is generating a ladder through which community members can contribute and be rewarded.

"We've just introduced a thing called 'Approved Helpers' – it's like a graduation scheme. You have to pass tests."

A ranking system offers badges of recognition as people become more involved, but the Approved Helpers put in even more effort, undertaking online tutorials.

Why would anyone bother? Because it opens the door to their earning more Payback points by offering quality support to the community. And giffgaff is also looking at how the graduation scheme could eventually lead into people getting a job at giffgaff.

Each Payback point is worth a penny. The record up to December 2012 was £16,000 earned by one member in one six-month period.

"It seems if you have people who are that involved in the business and that knowledgeable about the business, it makes sense to employ them."

Mike points out one of the team – Daniel, their app developer. "He was a member of the community who wrote one of the first apps that we had for iPhone. Half a dozen were written in the end, but his was the best one. So we employed him."

The giffgaff knowledge-base is also kept up to date as a wiki – with a team of "knowledge gardeners" volunteering to keep it tidy. They are entrusted with higher access to review and author. And that saves another two or three heads from the wage bill.

All this seems a powerful way to access community know-how and reward their input. The result is more accurate answers delivered more swiftly.

a powerful way to access community know-how

You have to ask – why doesn't the tax office (HMRC) give it a try?

"We ask ourselves why many different businesses don't do this? For me, from the experience of setting this up and getting it running, this shows the future direction that everyone is going to have to go eventually.

"The advantage of doing this for both the business and the customer makes it a win-win. It helps take dead wood out of an organization," said Mike.

So far giffgaff customers are described as members. And they are rewarded for active participation. But is there another step giffgaff can take toward making members the actual owners of the business? What are the limits for an organization which, at the end of the day, is a wholly owned subsidiary of a giant corporate?

"That all depends on your corporate governance. We are owned by a corporate so I think we've probably gone as far as we can. We can't become the full co-operative model."

Mike acknowledges that someone applying the Principle of Member Led more completely may be able to disrupt his model. But what he does have on his side is the benefit of all the corporate know-how – and deep pockets.

"Setting up a mobile network is an extraordinarily expensive thing," he smiled.

Healthy communities rarely grow themselves, either. Mike has a team of community managers whose job is to keep the community happy and healthy – primarily through one-to-one interactions with the super-users in the community.

One key learning is the importance of encouraging new members to participate. The rest of their time is spent making the community a warm and welcoming place.

"If you get this job right, instead of having to add more and more community managers at the center, you can rely on the community to manage itself and stop costs escalating," said Mike.

Another important aspect of the culture is that giffgaff offers members of its community great freedom and trust when it comes to the use of its brand.

"You have to be prepared to allow use of your name and logo. We are pretty free with allowing people to take graphics from our website and do stuff with it."

Again, there are limits. If you set up a site to pass yourself off as giffgaff to sell member-get-member SIM cards – and it misleads potential members, then giffgaff will get protective.

The Terms & Conditions lay out that you can't try and fool people by copying giffgaff.

And if the brand properties get used in an insulting or derogatory way – likewise, giffgaff would take action.

"But actually – that doesn't happen," said Mike.

"One of the things that I think have changed about branding is that traditional marketing departments used to think – and some of them still do think – that they are in control of their brand.

"The truth is that they have never been in control of their brand. They might have been able to control how it was printed, or what it looked like on a TV advert, but actually their brand is lived out by people in the street who talk about it, praise it, criticize it, or anything else. The living embodiment of the brand is in what people say to each other it is, and you have never been in control of that.

"These days, with social media, the same conversations are happening but now you can see them. And it makes it more obvious that you are not in control."

Mike contends there is no less control today, it's just that marketing departments are afraid that if they loosen their grip on the brand that somehow the brand won't exist – in the way that they would wish to define it.

"Brands these days aren't built by their definitions, they are built more by how you behave as a business."

For Mike the behaviors of the business must align with its Purpose. In the case of giffgaff it must show itself to be pioneering and collaborative – to provide a benefit.

"Pioneering? We're doing new stuff – pushing the boundaries. Collaborative? Working with our members. Benefit? That's our way of saying by doing the first two you actually create benefit for both the business and the member.

"For instance if we were working with members, the first thing we would be thinking is how do we provide a benefit back to the person who came up with the idea and how does it benefit our member base?"

Mike offered an example. If giffgaff sold mobile advertising – which it currently does not – or it sold access to anonymized member-generated data, its first thought would be to revenue share with members. If that proved impractical it would take the income and use that to keep costs down so that, again, members would benefit.

"That feedback loop which challenges us to ask 'how do what we do benefit us and our members at the same time,' is ingrained in the culture," said Mike.

Having a close connection to members through community acts as one giant "honk-honk" horn for that community to sound any time giffgaff wanders from its principles.

"If we do anything members don't like we hear about it really quick. From clicking the publish button on a blog post (we don't do press releases) it can be just three minutes before the feedback begins," said Mike. Within half a day Mike knows what the verdict is.

The team at O2 must be watching with envious eyes. Mike is getting fantastic customer information allowing him to shortcut innovation processes with more accurate delivery of innovation.

"They do look at that. And we are helping them actually. The trouble is the senior management can see it, but being such a large organization they find it quite difficult to put a change in quickly," said Mike.

When giffgaff has major decisions to make – if it doesn't have a really firm idea of what it wants to do – it goes out and talks to the community for suggestions. If it does have a clear idea – and some financial limits on that idea, then giffgaff will consult with that community.

"Before we make a price increase (or decrease – and that does happen) we'll do a consultation exercise. We did one in November 2012. We used to do unlimited data at £10 a month. Smartphone use meant the amount members were using was going up so we said: we have some choices to make.

"We SMSed everyone and emailed them, to say we were consulting. We blogged about it and then there was a discussion about it – on the forums."

Some may fear that would be giving away too much information to potential rivals.

"In this industry you can turn around a tariff price change – if you are determined – within a few days. We announced our intent to change price, by opening up the consultation, about a month in advance. So yes – we are at risk. But we think the advantages outweigh the risk.

"The advantages being that you get better feedback. And if you are open with your reasons then you can have a very rational conversation with your members. There are incredibly intelligent conversations that go on about cost base and regulation and everything else.

"Typically by involving your customers through the community they know what you want to do, they know why you want to do it and so when you actually do it, it's more accepted," said Mike.

The giffgaff also lives out the Principle of Shareability – and that is helping to drive its growth. They have a member-get-member scheme called "Spread giffgaff" with access to brand logos, and so on to be shared with peers.

"People like us anyway and recommendation will happen anyway, we just track this and reward it."

It is of course unlikely that friends will recommend what they don't like to their friends. Member-get-member should only work for products and services people like.

"We just give them the tools to make it easier for them to give their friend down the street a SIM card."

Each member has a personal URL (web page) which goes through to a personalized order page where if you blog about it, or update Facebook or Twitter about it and you use your personal URL. If someone clicks on your link as a result, you will be rewarded.

The principle of reward is writ large in the Ideas Board part of the community, too. It is here that Open Innovation comes to life.

"Anyone can go on there and enter an idea and then it has to get a certain number of kudos points from other members for us to consider it," Mike said.

Twice a month the senior team reviews the ideas that have reached the threshold and feedback on them. By making the cut you have earned kudos which will translate as a community reward. On occasion a manual bulk reward of points can be made as a thank you. And if the individual has the skillset to execute their idea they could be offered a job at giffgaff.

The Ideas Board has generated more than 9500 ideas. When the duplicates are taken out, about 10% of them have been implemented – about one every three days.

The more you are willing to be engaged, the more they will be engaged, said Mike.

"If Dell IdeaStorm (computer maker Dell's community collaboration platform) is the gold standard, then we beat that hands-down," he said.

"It is very useful. We get little things from 'you've got a typo on your website,' all the way to what we should do with our tariffing."

Some ideas appear at first, brilliant. But on investigation there are occasions when it's an innovation that giffgaff just can't deliver. The important thing is to provide feedback.

One issue with innovating in a crowd model is the representative nature – or otherwise – of those you are trying to innovate with.

"We have struggled a little bit because you don't necessarily get a nationally representative view about what your product should be from your community. By definition those heavily involved in the community are a certain type of person. They don't necessarily represent your base of members or your potential base of future members," said Mike.

He has acted on strong opinion from the community in the past – and seen the output bomb in the market. After trying this a couple of times in the early days of giffgaff, Mike has found it wiser to create a democratic route to getting ideas in front of his senior team, but for the business to act as the final decision-maker.

wiser to create a democratic route to getting ideas

"We'll commit to looking at an idea, but we'll make the decision and we'll tell you why we make that decision."

This raises wider questions about democracy and transparency. What is Mike willing to share? Where are the lines drawn at giffgaff?

"There's commercial stuff – we're a commercial organization. So we don't share details around profitability or the rates we pay O2 for our airtime and everything else. And that makes it difficult sometimes to consult on things.

"The other limitation is 'are we revealing too much to competitors?'"

Mike doesn't have specific rules about that but he is sure his competitors are among community members so knows he must tread relatively carefully.

One way around that is to bring trusted members of the community in, ask them to sign non-disclosure agreements and then tell them more about plans you have in mind. On occasion giffgaff do this and believe it works.

"We don't like to do it too much because our community is an equal community. We don't necessarily want to elevate any one member above another," said Mike.

The kudos system leaves that elevation in the hands of peers, rather than of giffgaff.

Mike isn't allowed to say how big the community is. But its millions of threads, 90-second response time, and 200,000+ Facebook Likes give an indication of valuable scale.

Despite this apparent success and despite making new products with his community, Mike still feels he is still – like most – trying to get to grips with making the most of social media.

"Where my head is at the moment is that, actually, if you focus on being a great company and offering a great service – and you focus on your own community, your members will naturally use the other communities they act in to spread the word about you.

"At the end of the day, things like Facebook are a social tool and the level of interaction people want from brands in that environment is pretty low," added Mike.

More than once during the course of our interview Mike refers to a belief system at giffgaff. It comes back to the Purpose Principle. If everyone knows what direction to head in you can share out more trust more widely. It has been an essential in the giffgaff community model because if you are not acting in line with your beliefs you will soon be found out.

At giffgaff part of the recruitment criteria is that potential staff should already be knowledgeable about the giffgaff community – and excited by it and the whole concept of collaboration with members.

That is a huge cultural driver. It puts the emphasis on the shared outcome, the shared journey, on collaboration rather than on the big man and his big idea. By selecting for those who collaborate first, the organization by necessity becomes collaborative.

For members, said Mike, although in a price-led business, when they are asked why they are with giffgaff they will agree with statements like "because they do the right thing" and "because I trust the business."

"We've done studies where we've compared ourselves on trust with the O2 brand and we are, for existing members, at a higher level than O2 is, and for our prospects we are not far behind."

Remember, giffgaff is only four years old. O2 is 11 years old – and has spent in the region of £1bn on marketing over that period of time. In that context giffgaff's trust scores are amazing.

Trust is even more essential to giffgaff than it is to O2: giffgaff has no contracts.

"Our members are free to go whenever they like. We measure member satisfaction and Net Promoter Score every day. On NPS we are very high. We are up there with Google and Apple which, for a telco company is extraordinary. Most telcos would be lucky if they got a positive score," said Mike. (NPS goes from -100 to $+100$. A typical telco is in the low 10s.)

The giffgaff lives a dislike of contracts which it believes it shares with its customers.

"Members don't like contracts when they feel tied into them and they're inflexible."

Mike says one of the places telcos make a lot of money is when your two-year contract may have ended – and you've paid off the hardware cost (of your smartphone) but they don't bother telling you the period is up – so you carry on paying at a much higher rate than your usage actually requires.

That's an aspect people don't like. But they do like the loan that you are effectively taking out when you choose an expensive device (your next smartphone). It's cheaper to buy your phone up front, but contracts spread that cost for those who don't have the spare cash to take that route.

By sticking in the SIM-only part of the market Mike thinks he only has access to about 25% of the market – since most people buy their SIM and their phone at the same time.

He was determined *not* to move into the hardware business unless he could do it in a way that gave members the things they like about contracts without the bad things.

"It's also a very complex area to get into. We are a very simple business and we want to stay simple," he added.

In October 2013, after a long period of consultation with its community, giffgaff announced its intent to supply phones as well as sim cards for the first time.

To keep things simple, just 22 handsets were initially listed. The only iPhones available were refurbished ones.

The simplicity principle extends to its service offering. While it offers a handful of "goody bags" which are one-month-at-a-time combinations of voice, data, and SMS, the average mobile operator may have tens of thousands of tariffs on its billing system.

"It's because of legacy tariffs which have built up over time – and they are enormously expensive to look after because each needs maintaining, managing, and messaging and everything else. We try to keep everything to an absolute minimum," said Mike.

Where does all this end up for giffgaff. What is their goal state? How much more collaborative, how much more democratic, how much more of an Open Business can the company become?

"There's a lot more we can do. We sat down maybe six months ago (late 2012) and said, we've been going for three years. We set the model up and thought deeply about it then. But what needs to move on? Because we need to keep on pushing the boundaries," said Mike.

"We think there's quite a lot more we could be doing with community engagement. We want to see more members in the office – and there are things we are working on which will enable us to do that – and get a steady flow of members in, helping us do stuff, giving them a nice day out, benefitting the business.

"And we've already talked about graduating members into employees," said Mike.

At this stage giffgaff is still focused on growth. In May 2013 it had yet to reach its minimum optimal size and was only around halfway along its planned growth trajectory. But it won't seek growth at the cost of its principles.

"There are always faster ways we could grow. We could distribute our SIM cards in Carphone Warehouse. We could get our airtime distributed through the supermarkets. We don't do either of those things at the moment because they don't fit with the way we want to work."

To continue to grow at the rate it would like, giffgaff has found it has had to turn to traditional advertising – a small shift from its reliance on the member-get-member model.

It's a trade-off. With a higher volume of advocacy the member-get-member model would work faster. It's yet to hit its critical volume.

"You have to jump-start the business. Since we've launched we have done some traditional marketing. We don't do traditional TV but we have done sponsorships. We do online display and pay-per-click ads. In combination with member-get-member, that gets us to where we need to be," said Mike.

"Ideally, in our goal state, we wouldn't need to do any of that traditional marketing. We would exist entirely on word of mouth alone. I don't think that's an unattainable goal. We can certainly take the marketing spend we have now and reduce it by 80%," he added.

Mike believes while in growth phase it isn't yet practical to talk about winding down his marketing spend. His business model has its minimum optimal size to reach. Yours may not.

Can the giffgaff model be applied elsewhere? Is an Open Business the right structure for others?

"If you take the basic premise from where we started: The existing market is toxic in the way they treat their customers – where else may that apply? Utility companies spring to mind," said Mike.

Imagine being able to buy a monthly supply of units of gas or electricity without signing up for locked-in contracts – a like-for-like disruption of the kind giffgaff has sprung on telco. It's not hard to see a business creating a new space right there.

Is that the kind of spin-off that giffgaff could target? Not just yet, says Mike.

"There are core skills that we have and core assets that we have. Our parent owns a mobile network, for instance. We don't have wholesale energy buying expertise."

But what of the incumbents in the utility sector? Could one of those have the foresight of O2, Gav Thompson, and Mike Fairman, and disrupt themselves? Could a platform provider offer month-by-month packages allowing switching to whichever deal suited you best that month, disrupting the traditional model still further?

If you are sitting in a large organization considering how you could apply Open Business strategy to achieve your breakthrough, Mike has some relevant learnings to share:

Be less precious about your brand

"You'll have a marketing department which is ultra precious about the brand because that's their job. But they need to relearn that, because it's not the way the world works anymore. Be precious about what your brand stands for, but less precious about signing off every blog post. Brands are built one brick at a time through your interactions – so that's what you need to be precious about."

Organize from the top-down

"If you are a big organization you do need to push [...] from the top down otherwise the basic difficulty of getting stuff done in an IT-oriented world will stop you being Open and stop you changing your systems in the way you need to change."

Embrace your customer

"There's a mindset thing. Getting that close relationship with your customers, through community, is different from the corporate mindset. The closest most people get to their customers in corporate land is when a particularly irate one turns up at the office and you let the security guard deal with it. Senior managers will have to get used to blogging – and not just blogging but actually reading the responses, and responding to them. They may have to do that at 8 p.m. when they are at home.

"I think it's a fantastic monkey on your back. Having your customers (member-base) there ready to clobber you if you do something wrong, keeps you on track."

Give it time

Today things are operating on an even keel. But it wasn't always that way. "It was a close run thing. There was an interesting time after we launched where we came within a month of being shut down. That was because we didn't have everything working as we would want. The community worked well but it wasn't of sufficient scale and we had a product which didn't have certain features that the market required, our pricing was a bit screwy and our awareness was low." Expectations had been set too high. The bean counters had expected linear growth, and were unprepared for the slow start hockey stick curve of many web-based businesses. "When we missed our targets for the first full year by 85% you can imagine the conversations I was having with the folk back at O2." Fortunately enough green shoots were emerging to indicate the hockey stick was arriving soon.

Today giffgaff is heading toward the good part of the hockey stick. It's gone beyond the early, and in retrospect justified, chatter that questioned whether or not giffgaff would make it.

The giffgaff model is born of a desire to make more of the world of Web 2.0, the world of everyone being a publisher and the shift in power that entails. If in media the power has shifted to the edge, what has that taught Mike about how a company should be organized?

"I think our model fits very well with the world as it now is. And as more people use social media, and turn to it first, then the market will come to us.

"I would be more concerned if I was sat in a more traditional company because the world is moving away from you," Mike warned.

Open future-proofs too

Mike says it makes the business more ready for further changes in usage patterns and customer demand. Compared to more traditional operators, giffgaff will learn of those changes faster and have a member-base ready to help them adapt to them more rapidly and more successfully.

Summary

Open Innovation is the integration of customers and stakeholders into the innovation process to share the risk and reward of developing new products, services, and marketing communications.

GOAL STATE / WORST CASE

Where does your business stand from 1 to 5?

Goal state (*scores 5/5*)

100% of developments in service, product or communications design are made in collaboration with people outside the organization in an appropriate co-creation process of shared risk and reward.

Worst case (*scores 1/5*)

All developments are made in secret and internally.

First **steps** …

If you estimate your organization is poor at this start by:

 Sponsoring an internal "hack day" in which teams with varying skills are brought together to create on-the-fly solutions for a charitable cause or to create a social good.

The process of identifying the right people to bring together, the skills they will need, and where you must look for them, will reveal much about how you could shift to more Open Innovation processes, including strategies which could involve those from outside the organization.

Think about the motivations of all parties and how you may be able to create similar motivations either through Purpose or reward. How could the Co-IP model referenced in this chapter work in practice for you?

chapter 7

Open Data

Definition

Making your data freely available to those inside or outside of your organization who can make best use of it.

Data.

Capturing it. Owning it. Interrogating it. Extracting it. Big Data. Personal data. Alan Moore, author of *Communities Dominate Brands* (futuretext 2005) and *No Straight Lines* (Bloodstone Books 2011), has described it as "the black gold of the 21st Century."

And like the rush for oil there has been a rush to discover, to tap, to own, to pipe, and to exploit it.

Open Businesses think differently about data. They know that in sharing what they "own" they create more value – both for themselves and others.

Like an idea, data has more value if it is shared.

Open Data can externalize and scale your R&D while reducing both the cost to innovate and (through engagement in the processes) the cost to market.

It is hard to talk about Open Data without referencing Goldcorp at least once (its story was first brought to my attention by Anthony Williams and Don Tapscott's 2006 book *Wikinomics*). The Canadian mining company was faced with rapidly rising costs for successful discovery of new sources of gold on its large landholdings. So, in 2002, it decided to share 45 years of proprietary geographical data with the world.

With a prize fund of $500,000 up for grabs, 1400 individuals and groups from across the globe sliced, diced, and otherwise interrogated the data to come up with the right sites to explore. They identified 110 sites – half of which the company had not known about. Since then four out of five have yielded significant finds.

The company's value before the contest? $100m. After? $9bn.

Open Data delivers crowd-sourced innovation. Simply from gathering and analyzing expressions of need or want through the thoughts people publish in their social media – for example – it is possible to identify new and emerging needs to service through products and services shaped to fit.

If you chose to track the mentions of tea-drinking in the UK in open social media (there are lots) you may be able to identify where and when people are drinking, for what purpose, to what benefit. Let us assume we see an uplift in late-night tea-drinking. It would be possible for a tea manufacturer to innovate a new low-caffeine "Midnight Tea" brand. And you would know where to market it, too.

Open Data distributes the management of the exponential growth in data sets (that Big Data thing). The scientific community is itching to take advantage of that with successes already scored such as the open and collaborative Human Genome Project (to map human DNA).

"Numerous scientists have pointed out the irony that right at the historical moment when we have the technologies to permit worldwide availability and distributed process of scientific data, broadening collaboration, and accelerating the pace and depth of discovery ... we are busy locking up that data and preventing the use of correspondingly advanced technologies on knowledge," says John Wilbanks, VP science, Creative Commons.

Our examples from both the *Guardian* and the UK government below further illustrate how sharing data garners greatest value from large data sets. In so doing, Open Data distributes the risk and reward of gathering data and innovating with it.

Understanding that data of many kinds is not something that is best owned by the corporation is a hard lesson for many executives. After all, many of us were sold on data being the key value we could derive from our Internet investments – particularly that data relating to our customers.

But there is a growing backlash against the idea of ownership of personal data of any kind. It is less about privacy, more about our desire to reclaim control about who we share what with. For customers Open Data means if anyone has to own data then it should be the customer not the corporation.

desire to reclaim control about who we share what with

Forbes reported in February 2012 that "CMOs (Chief Marketing Officers) must prepare for the next technology revolution." The revolution in question was the shift from organization-owned CRM (customer relationship management) processes to customer-owned VRM (vendor relationship management) as pioneered by Doc Searls – co-author of *The Cluetrain Manifesto* (Basic Books 1999) and author of *The Intention Economy* (Harvard Business Review 2012).

This "revolution" is, of course, far less tech/tool related than *Forbes'* headline suggests. It is far more attitudinal, demanding cultural shift.

The basic notion is that the customer gets to own their data and share it with whom they choose, to their own ends, and benefit (as opposed to the organization laying claim to customer data).

Washington DC-based tech company Personal is one example of the output of such a cultural shift in thinking. A web-based "personal vault," whatever you store (e.g., data, notes, files) through their products always belongs to you. You can give access to others – companies for example – for a period as and when it is useful to you. And you can stop that access at other times.

In many ways all this does is put the boot on the other foot. Do customers become "as bad as" corporations if we limit our sharing of data? The upside with VRM-style thinking is that at least the individual is making an informed choice about what and when and with whom they choose to share. Open thinkers may choose to share more openly – on the expectation of building benefit for themselves and others. Closed thinkers may prefer to accept the cost of that lost opportunity in exchange for their privacy.

This surfaces challenging questions about data ownership. What is the difference between our actions being recorded in a digital database – and them being recorded by our collective human memory?

Do human memories decay faster? Do digital ones do a worse job of delivering context (and therefore meaning)? These are the "technical issues." They are questions of effectiveness.

By what and by whom do we want to be remembered? Let's set aside for the moment that memory and data may be different things – that memory may be the story through which we understand the data stored in our and other people's collective memory. That applies equally to data stored in databases; it makes no sense without a story applied to it, derived from experience and with context.

We need to think about where on the scale of "wanting to be remembered by" we fit for the various relationships we have – from families to friends to favorite places. From, "ok" to be remembered by, all the way through to "desirable" to be remembered by? We want our friends and families to remember us. Is this different from data being stored in a database? If so, how and why? We want our favorite restaurants and hotels to remember us. We want society to remember us. We want posterity to remember us.

Throughout history the remembering has been done by other humans, creating context around the "data" of our lives through the stories they tell, write, record, and film.

So why not have Google storing your data? Why not Facebook? Why not the brands you consume? Perhaps they can record the source material more accurately than has been possible before. The stories that make the data comprehensible, that gives it its context, will still require humanizing.

Provided the data can be made available for re-use by others who could create still more value with it, should we really be concerned?

* * *

Open Data and Open Journalism

British newspaper – and global website – the *Guardian* opens its data as a matter of course. It is a key part of an "Open Journalism" approach which has seen it rise from being the ninth best-selling newspaper in Britain to the third biggest newspaper website in the world.

Its global stature was confirmed in summer 2013 when US defense contractor Edward Snowden chose the *Guardian* to help him blow the whistle on the PRISM program – through which the US government was claimed to be spying on citizens via the Internet.

Editor-in-Chief Alan Rusbridger is convinced his open-to-be-read-by-anyone approach (as opposed to the pay-wall model found at the *Financial Times*, the London *Times*, and the *Sun*, for example) was essential in delivering the global scale it now enjoys.

"And that is translating into commercial success in terms of our digital revenues," he told me.

The *Guardian* announced a "digital first" strategy in June 2011.

Alan is a long-time convert to the cause of Open. He believes it delivers better journalism through broader perspectives and a richer variety of sources – often from those closer to the action than news professionals alone can access.

Opening data provides a further way in which the *Guardian* supporters can both take value and contribute it.

In a world in which the growth of data appears unlimited but the ability to analyze it in-house remains finite, there are going to be more and more times when help from outside is essential to deal with the deluge. If your default is to share your data for others to create value with, their default will be to help you create value with it, too.

The *Guardian* has an Open Data resource on its website (www. theguardian.com) where it shares its data and makes it widely available through an open API, says Alan.

"Anyone can take our data, share it, do their own visualizations with it, analyze it and make their own judgments on whether or not we are reporting fairly, based on it. It's a very important part of what we do and helps win trust for our journalism," he says.

So, when in 2009 the *Guardian* called on its readers to help analyze 400,000 documents relating to the expenses claims of British members of parliament, they were able to recruit an instant team of 23,000 volunteers.

Their work delivered scoop after scoop for the *Guardian*, and a step-change in the accountability of MPs.

"That story is quite a good metaphor for the challenge facing news organizations. When 400,000 documents are released simultaneously it is beyond the capacity of any news organization to deal with it," says Alan.

"By recruiting 23,000 readers you make the task instantly more manageable."

The same benefit of scale from outside the organization was delivered again in the Arab Spring (from December 2010).

"You had simultaneous revolutions kicking off in seven or eight different countries. In terms of getting boots on the ground to cover all of these, there are very few news organizations which can deal with that.

"We had to pioneer techniques of open journalism in which we incorporate other sources and link to other people," he says.

"Journalism then becomes a slightly different job. We test the reliability and verify the people who we respect and then we harness them and what they do, to what we do."

The same thought process – of working with people from outside the organization for mutual benefit – applies today throughout the *Guardian*'s coverage.

"We are intensely interested in our readers' experience of the things we are writing about. A great example in the paper this morning (31 July 2013) is about 'zero hours' contracts," says Alan.

The paper reported how retail chain Sports Direct was employing 90% of its staff on "zero hours" contracts which meant they had no guaranteed hours each week and no holiday or sick pay.

"That's a piece of reporting," says Alan. "But then we have two pages of people telling us, 'that's my life, and I want to tell you about that.'"

The *Guardian* actively seeks support from outside in solving tough problems. When newspaper seller Ian Tomlinson was unlawfully killed during G-20 protests in London in 2009, the *Guardian* turned to its readers for help.

"We asked who could help us find the footage that showed how he was attacked," says Alan.

In other cases, Alan says: "You go on to Twitter and ask, did anyone witness something and you get many witnesses. You are there, through open reporting.

"There are numerous examples of us getting a vastly greater capacity by us harnessing other people's experiences of travel, food, fashion …

"We created the biggest environment site in the world by harnessing 28 other environment sites and putting it together in one hub.

"Wherever you look, it's now baked into our DNA – that we do all these things in an open way," he adds.

Alan says his push to Open would not work if it was just an edict from the top. His journalists have seen the benefits and now embrace Open, realizing they can give a better account of the world through it.

"They realize it makes their journalism better, which means our web traffic is going to get better, therefore the financial rewards will follow."

The *Guardian* is now a platform (for those who share its interests) as well as a publisher. But, Alan insists, it is not just a platform.

"If we were baling out of journalism and saying we are just creating a platform for other people that would destroy the point of the *Guardian*. What's really interesting is finding the right balance between publishing ourselves and being a platform for other people; and how the selection is made about whose voices are interesting, how you manage the debate ...

"All those are interesting challenges but the number one decision: Should you be Open or closed? Do you create a better journalistic endeavor by being Open? I think that is not a debate we have any more."

Alan says Open is leading to the creation of a different kind of news organization with a different kind of relationship with readers, one in which readers help shape what the *Guardian* is.

"It is one in which they will feel journalism is not done to them, or handed down from on high. It is journalism done with you."

That, he says, is a model which more accurately reflects both how society now is and how information will move around in the future.

This new relationship of sharing, Alan feels, is here to stay.

"There may be a handful of counter examples, where the fact that you have data and someone else hasn't may give you some advantage, but in the world of general news there's not much that you could get huge value from keeping to yourself. The greater value lays in openness."

Even so, he acknowledges that the journey can be a scary one to embark on.

"Can you be half open? When you start going down the road to openness it's difficult to start slamming stable doors," he says.

The *Guardian*'s first steps included having a "readers' editor" – someone to whom readers can complain, who is not the editor. Other businesses may call this a customer champion.

"No newspapers did it before in the UK, and none have done it since because it's a frightening thing, because you are losing control, your mistakes are going to be highlighted," says Alan.

"But I think the big picture is that in the world in which we live and the way that information now moves, all your mistakes are going to be uncovered. It's going to be on Twitter or Facebook.

"It's an uncomfortable thing to do but in the end, in the 21st century, it's better to do it yourself than have it done to you."

As a senior figure in the UK's media landscape, Alan regularly rubs shoulders with leaders of other industries.

"You sense they are having the same conversations. They are now much more about open-sourcing their R&D. They face the same conundrum we had with MPs' expenses; you can't analyze 400,000 documents with a staff of three.

"If you are Procter & Gamble, and Unilever are open-sourcing their R&D and you aren't, they are going to have an advantage, they are going to move quicker and be more responsive to customer need," he warns.

Alan's experience of Open is one which more efficiently delivers higher quality– and through Open Data and new relationships with readers, more trust.

"There is a power about Openness and transparency which is about trust, and participation, and diversity, and all the things we have been talking about. It's a very powerful idea.

"It has enabled the *Guardian* to grow faster than we have ever grown before and become larger than we have ever imagined.

"We are winning audiences who respect what we are doing and the money flows from that.

"The more you close yourself off, the less you become part of any of the conversations taking place, the less you'll be read, the less you'll be shared and the less relevant you'll eventually become," he concludes.

* * *

Open Data and Open Government

Central government in the UK has made efforts to replicate some of the thinking seen at the *Guardian* in its own Open Data movement.

Data.gov.uk shares public data with the intent of helping us understand how government works and why and how policies are selected. It includes over 9000 data sets from central and local government and other public sector bodies.

Importantly, it doesn't just share information, it shares the raw data. That means others can take that data and reuse it to create their own solutions, solving more problems, providing more answers than central government alone could if it relied only on its internal resource to interrogate the data.

The site hosts 69 case studies already – from Red Spotted Hanky (which uses openly provided data from the government-backed rail franchises to create an easier route to discount tickets for passengers) to Parkopedia (which uses Open Data to help drivers find nearby, low-cost parking).

The shift toward opening up government through data and other means was already well underway under the previous Labour administration. Prime Minister Gordon Brown (whose wife Sarah was and is an avid Twitter user) was a keen proponent.

Before being shown the door out of 10 Downing Street, Brown floated grand plans to "create innovation and 'personisation'" (or customer-centricity) in the delivery of public services. It seemed a huge enterprise. Brown said he was simply following the lead of business.

He said, launching the concept of "MyGov" in March 2010:

> Companies that use technology to interact with their users are positioning themselves for the future, and government must do likewise. MyGov marks the end of the one-size-fits-all, man-from-the-ministry-knows-best approach to public services.
>
> MyGov will constitute a radical new model for how public services will be delivered and for how citizens engage with government – making interaction with government as easy as internet banking or online shopping. This open, personalised platform will allow us to deliver universal services that are also tailored to the needs of each individual; to move from top-down, monolithic websites broadcasting public service information in the hope that the people who need help will find it – to government on demand.

MyGov was intended to replace DirectGov – and eventually morphed into Gov.uk – bringing all Government department sites (in theory) into one place.

Organizing websites is one thing, but shifting from a centrally organized model of government to one more focused on people is quite another. Some would say it's a mission on the scale of landing a man on the moon.

That's not because it seems almost impossible to do, but because the scale of change, the number of barriers to overcome are so large, that essentially the UK system of government, the control-from-the-center model that matched the industrial age, must be utterly transformed to match the demands of our Open age.

The Gov.uk initiative, for example, may be too focused on the technology, too little on the organizational change required to deliver the vision.

The win is that by shifting to more Open principles they can reduce the transaction costs of making things happen, turning a shared idea into an efficient "fit" through the bringing together of communities who care about the outcomes.

The fact that the technology enables transparency and connectedness like never before *is* critical. But the desire for, and organizational design for, transparency and connectedness (for sharing; for scale through participation; for search to discover and help us organize through connecting us and our data; and for enabling the always-on/not-always-available nature of the web) is the critical part – not the technology enabling it.

The opening days of the newly formed Conservative-Liberal Democrat coalition government in the UK in May 2010 revealed the financial world of pain we had all expected. It offered the single biggest opportunity we've yet had for fundamental, structural, governmental change.

The reality of the burden of the UK's record-breaking deficit and debt is that we must expect both a reduction in services *and* an increase in the amount we all have to contribute for them.

Open Government offers an option which can both better target resources *and* engage voluntary effort, which could have the net effect of both cutting costs *and* improving services. To reiterate: an organization should use its available resources to discover people who care about the same issues they do, bring them together, surface what they think needs fixing, and work with them (enable and join with them) to fix it.

If governing ourselves is all about ensuring resources are allocated as effectively as possible against the needs of the people (whether free marketer or command and control communist) then what the digital world has delivered is:

- A best-yet set of tools to discover the real-time needs of people
- A best-yet set of tools to engage with people
- A best-yet set of tools to enable people

Government – just as any business – could be redesigned to meet the needs of, and take advantage of, this Open, networked world.

Our current process of government, like mass media, has been built to serve the lowest-common-denominator needs of a mass production world. It results in one-size-fits-all policies, resource allocation (and, incidentally, political parties). That served the old world.

Today we can all find people who care about the same things that we do in real time. We can come together to discuss an issue. We can surface what needs fixing. And in engaging in the conversation we discover that we care enough about this thing that we are prepared to act to make it better (at least enough of us to make change). The government can be a platform for exactly this kind of collaborative innovation.

we care enough about this thing that we are prepared to act

Apply this to things such as policy development: Instead of relying on a small group of government-appointed experts beavering away, on any given subject we can:

- Expect that there are more people outside of government who care about the issue than inside
- Expect that there are more people outside of government who are more expert than those inside

An Open Government approach would open its doors to that freely-given expertise and insight.

Ongoing online listening can not only reveal where the people who care about each issue are (so you can invite them to participate), it will also reveal what the issues that matter are, where, and in real time. And it will reveal this in a long-tail rather than lowest-common-denominator way – that is, it will reveal all the niche interests that need serving, rather than the single biggest need.

The result of this is an Open Innovation approach to resource allocation – to make government services a better fit with actual, multiple, real-time needs. That equals less waste and more effective services for more people.

The other upside of this remarkable win-win is that in engaging people in the change they want, you get an army of volunteers to make the change happen: more people willing to take responsibility instead of leaving it to "the government" to sort out; more people willing to put their action where their conversation is.

And that means better services can be delivered at lower cost because more of us get involved in making, sharing, and delivering them. It is likely we would also end up restoring trust in government – as more people involve themselves in it.

I once bumped into Prime Minister David Cameron – just before the UK General Election in May 2010. We sat at adjacent tables in a London Starbucks. In our conversation about his lack of use of social media (he famously said "too many tweets, make a tw*t," though he is now on Twitter himself), I urged him to tell us what he actually thought, rather than tell us what he thought he ought to tell us. We would appreciate the honesty.

It seems politicians – with some rare exceptions (such as former Labour Deputy Prime Minister John Prescott, who has been an avid and active personal user of Twitter for many years) – see this as a step too far.

Most of us have no such qualms. We are quite happy to publish what we think – at least with a great deal more candor than the average politician. We don't even mind being proven wrong on occasion.

Unlike Prime Minister Cameron, many of us do publish what we think online – mostly via social media. We do so particularly about things we care about.

Things we care about include parliamentary bills. The Digital Economy Act rushed through in the wash-up of the end of the Labour government in early 2010 amply demonstrated how a community of purpose could discover one another and act rapidly around a social object – in this case a piece of parliamentary legislation with which they did not agree.

Similar communities of purpose exist around any issue – on or off the statute book.

How may the debate have been shaped had the pitiful number of MPs in the commons for the second reading of that Bill been able to see for themselves the thousands of comments that were being made, the excellent points raised by thousands of people on Twitter; the crowd-sourced brilliance of the nation our MPs are employed to serve?

The thousands of "small" voices online were drowned out by the physical presence of lobbyists in ministers' offices (as we will explore later in this chapter). Simply installing big screens in the Commons, the Lords, and the committee chambers showing all the comments about the day's relevant subject – collated and shown in real time for each debate – would at least place small voices in front of the right people.

place small voices in front of the right people

Open Government should not be attempted out of altruism. It should be done because it will improve MPs' decision-making effectiveness. It will improve our legislation.

MPs are generalists. They have to be. And for whatever given subject there is a community of purpose ready to come together to offer expertise and real-world experience far in advance of anything the House can muster on its own.

This is true of any business, too, of course.

We now have the social tools for communities of purpose to self-organize in rapid, ad hoc ways. The #debill campaign (which rallied against the Digital Economy Act and continued to fight it even after it was passed) organized 20,000 letters to MPs in seven days.

The Digital Economy Act tackles copyright infringement with a series of sanctions against alleged individual infringers and by blocking access to websites. Those fighting it felt it would result in innocent people losing Internet access and undermine the growth in public Wi-Fi. Their challenges meant it was 2012 before the Court of Appeal finally opened the way for the Act to be enforced. None of the sections relating to online piracy had been implemented even by December 2013.

It is easier now than at any time in history for people to discover other people who care about the same issue they do and to organize to make change.

Governments have the opportunity to join in. And they will if Tom Watson gets anywhere close to his way. Tom is the Labour MP for West Bromwich. He was also the first ever deputy chair of the Labour Party, a role he resigned from in July 2013 amid a row over the influence of unions on the candidate selection process for Labout MPs.

It was his third resignation from a front bench role since becoming an MP. Clearly a talent, we expect him to be fighting for the causes he is passionate about from the backbenches – and likely returning to a front bench role in due course.

In his resignation blog post (he remains a serving MP), he wrote: "I wish to use the backbenches to speak out in areas of personal interest: open government and the surveillance state, the digital economy."

Tom and I first met at a LinkedIn event hosted at the *Guardian* some years ago. Our conversation then marked him out as one of the rare politicians who understands the shifting sands on which government stands.

Today he believes the UK is presided over by the most closed government among Western democracies. It is a view that he feels more strongly today than 10 years ago. He is on a mission to change it.

He has always used social media to connect with his constituents and others. He won the New Statesman award for best use of new media in 2004 for his blog. He is very active on Twitter and was one of those central in the protest against the Digital Economy Act 2010.

Under Gordon Brown's premiership it was Tom who fought to make non-personal government data more widely available.

"I had always had an interest in technology. I almost ended up taking an IT degree but I ended up doing politics instead," says Tom, as we renew our conversation around a coffee table in his office at Portcullis House, Westminster.

In the last Labour government Tom served in the Cabinet Office where he set up the Power of Information Taskforce to examine the case for freer access to government data.

"As a junior minister your time is so limited you can only achieve a maximum of three big projects. You have to focus on priority policies. Mine was Open Data," said Tom.

"Wherever I looked across the public sector there were intrepreneurs who were trying to do great things and be imaginative and be creative with data.

"The irony was, that they were the problem."

All across the government new information assets were being created and some of the best people in the civil service were trying to monetize them.

"You had the meteorological office setting up separate businesses doing weather data, people trying to license business data, all that kind of thing. And, of course," says Tom with a heavy sense of irony: "Government knows best."

"I felt very strongly that what we had to do was throw all this data into the public domain, with no or minimum licensing, if achievable, and let the entrepreneurs out there go and do something with it to try and add value to the UK economy."

He tried to develop and share best practice with a competition called Show Us A Better Way which offered a £20,000 prize for the best idea for a website that used government data in innovative ways.

"It was essentially saying, 'Hello citizenry, come and tell these civil servants what great things you could do if we gave you this data'.

"What I didn't realize was that I couldn't just do this through force of political will – being unspeakably cruel to civil servants who didn't want to do what I wanted. There were technical, cultural, and legal impediments to overcome to get this data out there."

In short there was a lot of work still to achieve and even in 2008 Tom knew his time was ticking away ("It wasn't looking good for my party at the next General Election, even then.").

"I wanted to leave some initiatives that would be enduring. Firstly I thought if I create a civil service infrastructure around digital engagement it might start the process of culture change among the senior levels of the civil service; where these ideas that you could use new tools of engagement to open up government could be seeded."

The role of director of digital engagement was duly created within the Cabinet Office to drive that agenda.

He also started the Data.gov initiative about four months before he left office.

Among the more bizarre discoveries Tom made while working on the MyGov website initiative (referred to earlier this chapter) was that there was a DVLA (Driver Vehicle Licensing Authority) form on the site which you had to download, fill in, and then send in the post to the office in Swansea ... Where someone promptly copied what you had written on your form into a computer ...

A fix for this was on the to-do list of the project but it was seen as a low priority. When Tom discovered the data that there were hundreds of thousands of searches for this form each month, he was able to present the case that it be pushed up the priority list with immediate effect.

Tom's experiences in government and out in the last few years have given him a new imperative to act on Open Data.

"I am more strongly of the view today than I was 10 years ago that the UK has one of the most closed governments of all Western democracies.

"There is almost a civil service game to prevent people from getting access to information they need, and they go to extraordinary lengths to subvert the limited powers of the Freedom of Information Act," says Tom.

He points the finger of blame at the "circular and corrosive" relationship between the public sector, the tabloid press, and politicians.

"I'm part of this problem as much as everyone else. The idea that citizens can find out what's done with their tax dollars in their name, and challenge, to try to improve the way these services are done in their name, works. But there's an awful lot of political pain at the thought of tabloid stories appearing in the press (when failings are uncovered) – which means the political resistance just rises," he adds.

"You would not believe the number of hours I spent to try to get the value and inventory of the government wine cellar. It became a test of the Freedom of Information (FOI) Act for me."

Dozens of FOI requests followed from Tom – as did questions in the House of Commons. And the defenses went up.

"I was even invited on a private tour of the cellar (without being given the inventory). They went to massive lengths to try and shut me up."

Tom argues that if the government's position had been Open by default it would have published a list of these wines every year and it may have, perhaps, made a two paragraph story in a handful of newspapers.

But because the Foreign Office (which is in charge of the wine cellar itself) was hours away from being taken to court when they finally and reluctantly revealed details to the *Mail on Sunday*, the story became much larger.

"They had page spreads with bottles of wine at £10,000 each splurged across it."

The result has been a policy change. Because no serving politician can get away with glugging £10,000 bottles of wine, the stock is actively managed and bottles sold for profit, says Tom.

"We shouldn't need a Freedom of Information Act for something like this. If we were a proper Open Government like we see in Scandinavia they would list this on the website as a matter of course."

Tom is now trying to think about how the UK can go on the long march to Open Government.

"I didn't appreciate, until I was too late as a minister, that creating Open standards in data is probably the most important thing. Once the standard for a Bic pen in the Ministry of Defence is the same as a Bic pen in the Department of Business & Innovation, then you really are in action.

"I would hope that in 2015 (the year the next UK General Election is due), wherever the work on that has reached, and there's a shift in government, then we will spend even more time focusing on and accelerating that," says Tom.

Given how the web has disrupted much that has been centrally controlled in the past (such as media) does Tom think the role of government must change?

He believes there will always be a role for government in delivering core public services – due in part to complexity and the very high burden of quality demanded of them.

But, he says: "The debate of the last quarter century has been about the role private-sector partnerships can play in delivering services. The next iteration of that is how do you craft these services with your service users – leading on co-design.

"There's an enormous way to go on that, but quite an exciting agenda. If and when we get back (into power), I think there's another 25 years of brilliant co-design initiatives that we haven't even thought about yet," he says.

Political parties, like everyone else, have been struggling to come to terms with the digital age. Tom says for the first 10 years of the web parties liked to pretend it didn't exist. For the next 10 they tried to use it to broadcast propaganda.

"I think the next election will see digital being used to organize. And then we might actually crack it in terms of policy development," he says.

Tom turns back to the example of the Digital Economy Act.

"It was a real illustration of the limits of our parliamentary democracy. A lot of digital natives collectively organized in the online space against this bill. Because of the constitutional inadequacies of parliament, they were left particularly angry. That was because their voice was not heard in the shaping of this policy."

Proper soundings were not taken in the ordinary way because it was being done in the "wash-up" – the winding up of a dying parliament after it has been dissolved.

"It was an absolute outrage. An utterly disgraceful piece of legislation to go through Parliament in that way. And the person who pushed it through was Peter Mandelson (as Business Secretary).

"He should hang his head in shame for pushing through something that wasn't wanted in the country, was flawed in nature and which (as of July 2013) is in limbo because the current government doesn't know what to do with it," says Tom.

He believes parliamentary procedures must change to never allow the like again. Governments should not be allowed to introduce legislation once Parliament has been dissolved, he argues.

"It could only happen with the acquiescence of all Front Benches. The Lib-Dems, Labour, and the Tories collaborated to get this bill through. They did it because of massive lobbying pressure by big, old media publishing."

The "small" individual voices of the digital world – even though they came together quite effectively to say "no" – did not have the physical presence of lobbyists right in the faces of ministers.

The impact of that is still being felt across the digital community.

"It fostered a real sense of detachment between the elected and the electors. A lot of people gave up on government and politicians. And that's a tragedy because politics do matter and can make a difference to the world around you," says Tom.

One of the key lessons politics must learn from the Digital Economy Bill debacle is to listen where people are talking (most of the key conversation was online, the ministers were listening to lobbyists in their offices).

"Interestingly, since 2010 we have had about 400 MPs joining Twitter. There's now about 460-odd on Twitter. Some more active than others. But I now hear MPs saying, 'Are you sure about this bill? I've had three or four people DM [Direct Message via Twitter] me.' The idea that they know what DM means is a good sign," he smiles.

Tom believes the adoption of social media by increasing numbers of our representatives may have more of a cultural impact than we have yet realized.

One of the most culturally significant impacts of data and our increasing ability to crunch more and more of it, are the questions of privacy it raises. Tom believes the concept is in a significant state of flux and will continue to be at the center of debates for the next half-century as we come to terms with the potential for ever-greater knowledge about everything everyone does.

"I look at my son, who is eight, and think he is going to live his entire life with a digital imprint he won't be able to erase – probably the first generation doing that.

"In one sense I'm an optimist. We will have to be a more tolerant society."

We will have to accept that people do daft things on occasion, that a drunken picture on Facebook isn't a reason not to employ the candidate in front of you, for example.

But he also sees a darker side. One in which countries spy on their citizens.

The US PRISM project, which was reported to have been tapping into digital conversations on a global scale in June 2013, revealed the truth of the dark scenario.

"The honest truth is right now (at the end of June 2013) I have no idea what data the US and UK collect and don't collect. I have no idea how it's authorized and I don't know what it's used for. And I'm a former defence minister and Cabinet Office minister.

"I would imagine that most government ministers would have no idea about these programs nor how they are conceived, what they do, what good has been done with them, what harm has been done with them," says Tom.

It is unsustainable from a political point of view, he says, that Cabinet ministers are kept in the dark about what is done in their name.

Cabinet ministers are kept in the dark

Both unsustainable politically – and less likely too, as and when government becomes more open.

So what are the next steps of Open Government – from the point of view of a senior politician who may have a significant role in making it happen?

Tom stood at the last election on a manifesto which called for more Open Government, reforms to copyright and freedom of expression, which gives us a steer. But he's keen to caveat the following with the disclaimer that this is neither official Labour policy nor a manifesto commitment. However:

"I would like to show intent by giving some early wins to people who are very interested in Open Government.

"There are early wins we can give with the Freedom of Information Act."

First, the remit should be extended so that any provider of a public service paid for by the tax payer is also subject to the Act. This becomes important in the context of widespread privatization of Government services such as the NHS and Free Schools.

"The Department for Education currently advises people setting up Free Schools on how to constitute themselves to avoid falling within the remit of the Act. You can get all sorts of information out of a comprehensive in the state sector and next to nothing from a Free School – and as a parent, that's not right."

This extension to all public service providers, alone, would be a radical addition to the Freedom of Information Act.

The other shift he would advocate is small changes in the rules to ensure organizations can't prevaricate in their responses to FOI requests. They currently must respond within 20 days. But with appeals, they can string this out for years, says Tom.

He would make changes to ensure appeals happen faster – before those chasing the information get put off and give up.

"Both these small changes give power back to the citizen and take it away from faceless bureaucrats," he says.

If he has his way, that would happen within the first 100 days of a new Parliament.

The other step he would seek to take is larger.

"The default position would become that everything is in the public domain unless you specifically select not to make it public domain – and if you do then you have to justify why a piece of information mustn't be out there.

"I have a sense that the new leadership of the Labour Party include much more innate digital users such as Dr Stella Creasy (Shadow Minister for Crime Prevention) … these are the people who may be able to lead the cultural change to make that happen," says Tom.

As the digital natives invade all organizations they bring change with them. Why should government be any different?

* * *

Open is the new normal – and so is disruption

Sharing data, providing access to data sets, is one, very good, thing. But with all forms of information, a shared interface, an information architecture, is essential to deliver the greatest benefit. Codifying a set of rules around writing, for example, helped more people create with it, understand with it, and connect with it.

Providing more perspectives on that data may prevent the risk of human bias in interpretation that large data sets tend toward.

As data scales so does the ratio of noise to signal. But the act of selection of signal adds risk of bias. Bias is a dangerous thing when you are trying to make predictive models, according to the work of *The Black Swan* (Random House 2007) author Nassim Nicholas Taleb, and of Nate Silver – author of *The Signal and the Noise* (Penguin 2012).

The more complex the predictive model, the more restricted and limited it is by the biases of its creators, and the greater the room for disruption from a "black swan" (catastrophic, unpredicted) moment. It is closed to new possibilities, built to deliver understandings based on the possibilities of the past. The one certainty is that, given time, most things regarded as extreme will happen. Ask the dinosaurs.

most things regarded as extreme will happen

The more the amount of information we have at our hands exceeds our ability to process it, the more likely we are to fall back on the default shortcut of bias. Played out at a societal level this amplifies – leading to polarization.

This resort-to-bias is a natural human state – a shortcut which saves us time and has served us well through most of evolution. We seek information that supports our natural biases rather than that which counters it.

Some argue this selective bias was amplified by the arrival of the printing press and the explosion of information it delivered. They see (alongside the Cambrian event of the Renaissance) a causal link to polarization that gave us a century of religious war and persecution.

The risk of our latest information explosion – the Internet – is a new and potentially more radical divergence of thought – left and right. Both sides will have the potential to prove themselves "right" with the data – according to their biases.

One magnificent defensive shield against this, then, is the work and ambition of the Open Data Institute. Promoting more interoperable data means more people can access it, understand it, and act on it – potentially acting as a dampener on extremes of bias, and offering a level of protection against one bias becoming dominant.

Sir Tim Berners-Lee's great contribution to the web was in creating a standard all could share. He kicked it off with the shared protocols of the web and has continued to support it with his work at the World Wide Web Consortium (W3C), "a web standards organization ... which develops interoperable technologies to lead the web to its full potential."

As Tom Watson MP puts it: "If only we'd had Sir Tim when we were building the European rail network, we wouldn't be screwed by the time we got to Dover ..."

Now, with co-founder Sir Nigel Shadbolt (a fellow government advisor on Open Data, professor of artificial intelligence, and head of the Web and Internet Science Group at the University of Southampton), he is attempting to replicate the model with the Open Data Institute.

At the 2013 G8 summit hosted in the UK, the Open Data Institute (ODI) launched its Open Data Certificates – with the support and agreement of the leaders of the world's biggest economies. A week later the G8 agreed to its own Open Data Charter.

UK Deputy Prime Minister Nick Clegg said in his closing remarks at the G8 event that "Open is the new normal" – expressing one of five fundamentals agreed by the G8 governments – a commitment to "Open by Default" when it comes to government data, which will come as music to Tom Watson's ears.

That was followed at the end of June 2013 by the announcement of Open Government Licence v2.0 from the National Archive. It is an open license which allows the use and re-use of a wide range of national and local government information with few limits, for commercial or personal use and without charge. You have to acknowledge your source (without claiming endorsement by that source) and commit to excluding personal information.

It was launched only after consultation with the Open Data community.

While the Open Data movement has been growing for over a decade, the ODI is the world's first and only institute focused on ensuring data becomes truly Open, says its CEO Gavin Starks – a man with a rich background, which includes developing Internet research tools, raising venture funds, working with the Jodrell Bank Radio Observatory, co-creating the harbor co-operative he lives at on the Thames and releasing his own album: *Binary Dust*.

Live since 1 October 2012, the ODI was several years in the making with much effort from Sir Nigel and Sir Tim to attract the funding.

Gavin suggests that the fact it was signed off under the previous Labour government in the UK, and re-signed off by the current Conservative-led coalition, reveals how its value is recognized across party political lines.

It is intended to deliver triple bottom-line value – economic, environmental, and social – a mantra increasingly important to both governments and the largest of PLCs. Triple bottom-line thinking is helping reframe the challenges facing the planet – complex and inter-related challenges the London-based ODI feels its work can help solve.

> "Our mission is catalyzing the evolution of Open Data culture.
> "Open Data is a cultural phenomenon like the web. It feels very much like the early days of the web in that people are excited about its potential – but talking about it more than doing something with it."

To trigger more people being able to do more with it, Gavin explains: "We need more of a systems approach, where externalities are part of your modeling for social investments and environmental equity."

It is exactly this form of connectedness that URLs and http protocols gave the web.

Open Data is not just about the release of individual data sets, health, law, housing, or whatever – it is about how they act together. And then it is about how they act when combined with weather, water, farming, etc. Open Data can be the key to identifying benefits by combining them all – through creating and promoting standardization.

"One of the reasons the web works is that there's a standard way of publishing – a structured way of creating and storing information. We help data publishers understand what they are publishing, and to organize that around the needs of users," says Gavin.

"By creating a mechanism for sharing, arguably, the web is the most successful information architecture in history," he says.

And look what happened to the web once that mechanism was enabled. It is hard to predict what Open Data could yet deliver for society by building on an emerging web of data.

And, Gavin insists, this is not about dictating that there must be only one way of publishing information. APIs (application programming interfaces) of the kind Twitter shares to enable an ecosystem of developers on its platform will have value where data needs to be queried more regularly, for example. But a straightforward CSV file (comma-separated values) of the kind pumped out by basic spreadsheets can be an equally valid source of Open Data.

According to the ODI, the key to good Open Data is that it:

• Can be linked to, so that it can be easily shared and talked about
• Is available in a standard, structured format, so that it can be easily processed
• Has guaranteed availability and consistency over time, so that others can rely on it
• Is traceable, through any processing, right back to where it originates, so others can work out whether to trust it

Gavin is keen to stress that Open Data doesn't mean your personal details get shared – at least not without your explicit, informed, opt-in.

For example, there was no need for personal data sharing when the National Health Service published its data about what drugs had been prescribed where and when.

"We looked at statins (a class of drugs which aim to reduce cholesterol levels), looking at prescriptions and where a generic rather than patented version of the drug could have been used.

"We helped convene domain experts from health and a data analytics company and found that over £200m could have been saved on just one class of drugs."

Part of the role the ODI has set for itself is to promote the value of Open Data to the mainstream. To that end it took its learnings about the savings to be had in the NHS to the likes of the *Financial Times* and the *Economist*. Having a good Open Data story to tell is essential, Gavin argues.

The NHS story allowed them to raise additional funds with which to apply their process to the rest of NHS prescriptions. This looks likely to provide evidence for £1.5bn to be saved.

"There aren't enough good stories that have been told about the power of Open. There is a global push towards Open but we are still building the evidence base.

"It's like the early days of the web. We had many efforts at indexing and people trying to make a business out of mapping the web. But it took us a long time to get Google," says Gavin. "I would be very surprised if there aren't billion dollar companies in health or insurance built on Open Data in the future," he adds.

There is much that data can do for us. But it won't do it alone. Gavin points out that when radio was invented there were many utopian stories written about how it would bring the world together and solve our problems. The same happened with TV, and the web, and now with data.

"There is a belief in a technocratic future in which the data will save us," he says.

"But this is just another set of tools, another set of insights. We can make better decisions but we still need to make the decisions."

Countries and organizations and academics are all publishing data using different mechanisms. The ODI is standardizing some of the questions that need to be asked when compiling and publishing that data: What is the structure? How is it licensed? Does it include private data, for example? Applying the same set of questions across all existing data sets will make the information more discoverable in the first place – in another parallel with the early web.

Gavin says: "Pages emerged, then the tools to discover them, then those to help you organize them. Applying the same to data means you'll be able to find it, understand what it is and use it more easily – that's the objective of Open Data."

The web stumbled on for several years before the standards of W3C emerged. Open Data has a head start. It had access to global collaboration in developing the Open Data Certificates in the first place.

Then, thanks to the track records of the likes of Sir Tim and Sir Nigel, it was able to secure £10m of public funding in the UK from the Technology Strategy Board (the UK innovation agency) and $750,000 from the Omidyar Network (the philanthropic investment firm established by eBay founder Pierre Omidyar and his wife Pam).

A number of corporations have taken out membership – including Virgin and Which.

But few new bodies (with ambitions to act as a bridge between the commercial and non-commercial) can have hoped for the level of international support and recognition that the ODI had conferred on it by the G8.

"To have Open Data on the agenda of a G8 meeting and have them sign up to an Open Data charter is astonishing. It's nothing to be underestimated. It really elevates us in the political sphere and now our political leaders are helping to drive this forward," says Gavin.

"When you have the President of the United States signing an executive order demanding that all government data is machine readable, then it's clear we have turned a corner.

"We are in a new era in which people can use Open Data to generate insight, ideas, and services to create a better world for all," Gavin enthuses.

It doesn't stop with sign-off. The ODI is now entering into a two-year program with the World Bank to train world leaders to the point at which they can develop their own Open Data policies.

So far, 20 countries have expressed interest. Yes, including post-PRISM (the alleged program by intelligence agencies to spy on citizens' Internet use) USA and UK. Liberia, Indonesia, and China are all on board, too. And 27 companies have signed up as members – including Quanta Computing of Taiwan.

The potential of the web a year after the birth of the W3C wasn't on the political agenda. The potential of Open Data, a year after the arrival of the ODI, most certainly is.

Not everybody is leaping on the bandwagon. Even 20 years into the life of the web, the music and film industries are still slow to adapt to the rapid change in consumer behavior enabled by new technologies, says Gavin.

"Some companies see the web as part of their future. Others just see risk. The risk of not engaging is greater than the risk of engaging. The same is true of Open Data," he adds.

"Transformation never comes without disruption. It's going to take strong leadership (which we have at least from our political leaders) because if Open is the new normal, then so is disruption," warns Gavin.

The political leadership is already bearing fruit.

"I heard … that four African leaders will publish all the mining/extraction contracts for their countries and allow people to map where the money is going into their countries and where it is going out."

Imagine the questions that may raise.

In Open Data businesses face a force with as much potential to disrupt as the web had. So what advice does the CEO of the ODI have for those watching the tide rise?

"I'd start by asking what data do you produce which may have value to others? If you aren't using it I would open it up immediately. Even just doing that will be a step towards creating deal flow."

You start the back scratching. Expect your back to be scratched in return.

"If someone else can find money in that data, then let's discuss the commercial models under which you continue to make it available. You could license it out, for example.

"I'd also look at what data is going to become available. What will happen when what I think of as my proprietary data gets made available for free by a competitor? What do I need to change about my business to account for that?

"What new data sets are going to be made available to create value for me and my customers. How can I plan for that?

"I'd also be asking what happens as the storage of data is commoditized – bottoming-out at close to zero. This is going to really transform and disrupt. It will radically alter the access to market – democratizing many."

New businesses based on Open Data are being incubated by the ODI. One has already closed its first round of funding, another has just closed its Series A funding round.

Gavin has no doubt successful businesses can be built on Open Data.

"We're looking at future business models. Some have similar shapes. Some have different ones. You have to re-engineer how you work to deal with the change.

Owning data is a model for the old, closed world. Sharing in its bounty is for the new and future Open world.

Summary

Opening up your data can identify new business opportunities, share research and innovation costs, and align you with a global movement which looks set to have as great an impact as the web itself.

GOAL STATE / WORST CASE

Where does your business stand, from 1 to 5?

Goal state (*scores 5/5*)

Any data generated or collected by the organization is made publicly available where there is a possibility that sharing this data can create additional public good. For example, APIs. All data is searchable internally and externally. Ideally all data has achieved Open Data certification.

Worst case (*scores 1/5*)

Data is jealously guarded and kept secret. Competitive advantage is believed to reside in ownership rather than collaboration.

First **steps** …

If your organization scores low here's how you can start the ball rolling:

1. Identify the data sets you have available.
2. Assess which appear to have little value to you.
3. Make these available openly.
4. Consider corporate membership of the ODI to access further support.

chapter *8*

Transparency

Definition

Decisions, and the criteria on which they are based, are shared openly.

Transparency and Openness are, for many, synonymous: You can't have one without the other.

And it's almost impossible not to be heading hard and fast toward Open once you choose to be transparent.

But it is also the principle which strikes most fear into the hearts of business leaders.

We have become used to keeping secrets. The value we place on "intellectual property" (IP) has skewed our approach to this. It has driven us to place locks on our filing cabinets, password protections on our computers – levels of security above and beyond that of most personal bank accounts in many cases. We have built from a principle of opacity first.

We do this because we assume there is competitive advantage in blocking our competitors' view of what we know. Often we see that competitor within our own business.

On occasion there is a secret sauce – an Irn Bru recipe held in the head of one person; The Colonel's secret blend of herbs and spices; The formula for Coke.

The problem is that most companies extrapolate from this that if some IP is worth locking behind closed doors, then so is all IP. And that's an over-reaction of monumental proportion which leaves the business of knowledge management in the hands of your IT department and your facilities manager.

Not only is this a false "if-then" logic, but given how much of the value of your business resides in the good and distributed decisions of your people, it's an expensive mistake.

At the very least you must begin to address that balance between secrecy and knowledge. Start by thinking how to place the distribution of knowledge in the hands of those who need and use it.

Transparency delivers a range of benefits:

It ensures the organization makes decisions consistent with its Purpose, in line with its declared beliefs or intents. If you say you are going to do something and you are transparent in your reporting (and in our connected world you may not have a choice about this anyway) then being transparent makes tracking and governance more effective.

It can drive incremental improvement in the performance of the business. Being transparent means you have a crowd of interested observers to provide checks and balances to protect and direct you.

It can mean you attract the right employees, partners, and customers. In opening yourself up you reveal the realities of the business, and that makes it easier to match up with the best-fit people and businesses for you.

It can reduce the impact of unpopular decisions by virtue of being honest and open about the rationale behind them. Being open in your decision-making builds affinity and trust with customers and suppliers

And it corrects imbalances, and ensures the relevant information is shared among teams to create a fairer and more productive workplace.

And why is all that valuable?

Well, in the case of Walmart (which turns over $444bn a year and employs more than 2m people – not including those in its supply chains) the giant retailer believes transparency will help it achieve its sustainability goals.

It has launched a sustainability index to openly show how its supply chains can be judged against the following criteria:

• To be supplied 100% by renewable energy
• To create zero waste
• To sell products that sustain people and the environment

Members of relevant sustainability lobbies sit on key decision-making bodies within Walmart to hold the company to account.

In the UK the group is represented by the Asda retail chain. Its sustainability strategy will deliver £800m in savings by 2020 (source· Walmartstores. com).

Interestingly, in the first Havas Meaningful Brands Survey of June 2013, Asda out-performed all its direct rivals to be ranked fourth in the UK (only behind Clarks, Marks & Spencer, and Google). The survey ranked brands for their impact on quality of life across parameters including health, happiness, financial, relationships, and community.

Walmart is writing large its desire to be transparent. But how far would or could you go?

Imagine being transparent about what every member of staff is paid, for example?

"It would be chaos. The back-biting, the squabbling, the ill-feeling would cause a melt-down," shiver those who fear transparency.

Yet we expect exactly this of our politicians. We expect exactly this of the boards of PLCs. Look up any senior executive in the BBC on the web and you'll not only find their salary details, you'll also find PDF files to download of their expenses claims.

South African entrepreneur Arthur Attwell insists on everyone on his team knowing what everyone else is paid – even though he says many an Open Business advocate would think him crazy.

Arthur, a fellow of South Africa's Shuttleworth Foundation – an experiment in open philanthropy which provides funding for innovators who aim change the world for the better – worked for multinational publishers Oxford University Press and Pearson in the early part of his career. What he noticed was the tendency to close up; to shift toward opacity, that we have described above.

"The thing that worried me most of all was that the staff didn't actually understand what made the company tick. I didn't recognize that until I had a particular manager who was absolutely dedicated to making sure that all his managers really understood the finances of the company.

"I was 22 at the time, probably promoted above my abilities, sitting in with these guys going through in-depth company accounts," said Arthur.

"After a few weeks I realized that I now felt more empowered to do a good job, knowing what the company needed from me, than I had experienced at any time previously in my, at that point, very brief career."

He had got his first taste of the benefits of transparency. It's a taste he liked and which has driven the way he has set up three of his own businesses – in each case dedicated to being Open Businesses.

"What I had discovered was that the key to productive employees were people who really understood the finances of the company.

"So many pockets of information are kept away from staff – particularly salary information. Any kind of secrecy in a company dis-empowers the staff. If you hold back information, if they don't have the information they need, they can't do a good job," says Arthur.

"Secrecy comes from a sense of fear among decision-makers that the staff can't handle all the information that bosses can. I've found that isn't true."

Today Arthur is focused on his latest venture Paperight (where he is founder and CEO). It's a team of just eight people right now.

"I suppose my policy of radical transparency about salary is much easier to manage in a small company like ours. But I would like to think the principles could be the same for a large company."

Arthur thinks so because he believes that salary secrecy is "like a grenade waiting to go off in your business."

"It's a ticking time bomb because what happens is that when someone gets unhappy for any reason (maybe they have a colleague they don't like, or they feel bullied or they feel over-worked), they go looking for the salary information.

"Because it's been kept from them they feel it could answer for them why they are unhappy. Is it because they aren't paid enough or their colleagues are earning more?" says Arthur.

The secrecy makes it more interesting. "You are planting something for people to go looking for."

The problem is, you can't hide it. All it takes is a few beers after work and before long you know what your colleague is earning.

They then think the solution to their problem is what they are earning.

"They'll think, 'if I was paid more I'd be able to put up with the over-working or the bullying,' or whatever was making them unhappy.

"Making salaries transparent means you take away the possibility of that grenade blowing up in your business," says Arthur.

It also puts effective pressure on the leader of the business.

"I am forced to justify my decisions about salaries if everyone knows what those decisions have been. It's very easy as a manager – if salaries are hidden – to pay people radically differently based purely on how well they negotiated at their job interview or on your own whims and prejudices about that person's value," says Arthur.

"It forces me to be fairer – and that in turn inspires trust in me from my team."

The third benefit is that transparent salaries mean you have to be able to justify your salary to your peers.

One valuable output for an Open Business is that the company becomes less hierarchical as it is inevitably more flat in its earning levels.

Arthur isn't hung up on transparency for its own sake.

"I sincerely believe you get a productivity boost from people who properly understand their importance to the company and the role they play. So many people – even unconsciously – think that they are just a tiny cog in a big machine."

That leads to an attitude with which it doesn't really matter whether or not they put in one hour's work or 20 in any given day. Ultimately, they feel, the big machine will roll on without them.

"They feel an alienation from the products of their work," says Arthur.

Without transparency it's difficult for people to find meaning in their work. And without meaning there is little ambition and even less joy.

With it, people understand their value, they feel their work has meaning.

"I genuinely feel I get more productivity this way," says Arthur.

He also believes that being transparent with the partners he works with will build trust.

"I find it very disturbing when I work with partners who hold back information from me that I think I need to be able to collaborate properly," says Arthur.

In other words, being transparent results in a collaboration bonus – delivering more partners more able to collaborate effectively.

A further transparency bonus is the one this CEO gets from not having to focus time, energy, and resource on protecting IP.

"Because we don't have any internal secrets I don't have to waste any time protecting internal secrets. A lot of companies have to spend a great deal of time and effort trying to ring-fence pieces of information from people in the company and from people outside.

"We don't worry who knows what – we just plough on ahead," says Arthur.

He does not do this blindly. He is fully aware that his business could get side-swiped one day by a competitor which gets some information Paperight lets out.

But, he says: "I would rather cross that bridge when I come to it than be paranoid about it all the time."

Arthur would rather carry the tiny risk of that side-swipe for the benefits of transparency.

"You act on what you know, not what's possible. And what I know right now is that I get better trust and productivity from my staff today by being transparent," says Arthur.

Arthur's business is all about broadening access to information. In this context being anything less than transparent would make little sense.

Paperight is, at its core, a rights market place. That is made real by turning a network of photocopy shops into print-on-demand bookshops. In South Africa (and other developing countries) bookshops are a rarity. Access to the web is far from universal, too. Even where they do have access online the majority don't have credit cards to buy online. So scaling the number of cash payment book outlets is a valuable contribution in broadening access to essential information.

"What does exist in every town and village in the developing world is a photocopy shop. They are little economic hubs of activity for numerous reasons. They are also de facto producers of books, often illegally – photocopying books where they aren't available otherwise."

Arthur cites the example of Khayelitsha – near Cape Town – which is reputed to be both the largest and fastest growing township in South Africa with a population of (he estimates) around two million people. In it there are no bookshops – but five photocopy shops.

"We provide the content that these photocopy shops provide for their customers and essentially try to bring them into the legitimate book distribution chain by having them pay license fees to print books out," says Arthur.

The shopkeepers register on Paperight.com and when a customer comes in and asks for a book they can download and print the book out. Paperight takes a small license fee from a pre-paid account, and takes its cut and pays a fee to the publisher.

There are 180 stores in South Africa and a handful in other locations, 80 publishers are signed up. The majority of publishers are African but there are around 20 UK and US publishers signed up, too. They include O'Reilly Media and there are advanced conversations with major romance and two academic publishers in the US and UK.

One of the principles Arthur is working to is that of opening up the market.

"We are opening up the book selling industry to anyone with a printer and an Internet connection. That's important to us and it does have practical implications," Arthur insists.

In a challenge to the end-to-end control thinking of most production businesses, Paperight has no control over the finished quality of the product and therefore no control over the end-user experience. No minimum-standard demands are made of the photocopiers, the ink, the paper, the binding.

"If you can print something out, you can sell our books. We don't mind if its black and white, stapled, or ring bound. That comes with downsides but it's a decision we've made on principle – because we want the market place to be open to anyone.

"We don't control the customer experience, but that's a trade-off that I'm willing to take because the open-ness of the marketplace is more important than creating barriers to entry," says Arthur.

Best practice is shared and that will eventually be made into an operations handbook which will act like a franchisee guide for anyone wanting to run a great copy shop. It'll be published under an open license and users will be able to take from it what they choose.

That will help replicate the success stories. While currently the average number of books sold each month per outlet is as low as two, there are some which are selling closer to 150 per month.

While recalling that books sold in this on-demand way represent the only offline access to that book for that reader, it may come as a surprise to find in many cases the cost is lower for a one-off print than is charged for the mass print-run originals. The price is fixed by three things: the license fee set by the publisher (of which Paperight takes 20%); the per-page price charged by the copy shop, and, of course, the length of the book.

Typically a higher education textbook can come out cheaper – particularly since the buyer may select only 200 of the 800 pages as relevant to their needs. The model allows a little of the per-track disaggregation that iTunes delivered to the music industry. The average saving across the range of Paperight books is 20%.

The contracts used – for either copy shops or the publishers who use the platform – are designed to be as simple – and transparent – as possible. They are short and use plain language. Clarity is transparency.

"Importantly they are non-exclusive and you can cancel any time.

"It's an important principle of Open Business to me that the participants can walk away at any time. For example, if I use Google for my email/spreadsheet/document services I can download all my data, close it down, and walk away with everything," Arthur states.

The same applies for Paperight. The publishers and store owners can switch off their access and walk away at any point they choose. They aren't locked into anything.

This challenges a lot of assumptions about business – particularly for those who place valuations on businesses. The ongoing contracts you have are calculated in the net worth of the company. In reality, what that assessment is really seeking to measure is the strength of business ties through which more revenue will flow. Contracts guarantee that revenue. But for how long? The moment you have to enforce a contract is the moment you know the relationship is irreparable.

Increasingly we are seeing trust is more important. And trust doesn't refer to the contract.

"It leads to some interesting conversations. Our contract allows publishers to cancel pretty much immediately and for ANY reason," Arthur explains.

This confused the legal team at one publisher. First they asked if *X* happened, could they cancel?

A: Yes. For ANY reason.

They went away again then thought of another contingency. What if *Y* happened?

A: Any reason.

And if *Z* happened?

A: Yes.

It was surprising to them that a business would be so willing to rely on the quality of its behaviors and performance to maintain a relationship, rather than a contract.

quality of performance maintains relationships – not contracts

Building and maintaining a culture of transparency depends on recruiting people who believe in the value of working in this way. Everyone on the current Paperight team is involved in interviewing candidates. Everyone has a say. But that's a two-way street. Candidates get to experience everyone they may be working with.

"That's easy to do when you are small – and critical in getting the right people for us," says Arthur.

But he does have a way in which he hopes to be able to scale the approach.

The job descriptions he offers people are just three lines long. There is no task-by-task list of things to do every day.

Everyone must have the ambition to own their space in the company.

"That's why we don't have job descriptions in the conventional sense. We have a maximum three bullet-points of functional responsibility. Some people have just one or two," says Arthur.

"What that means is the things in those bullet points are your problem. It means people have to engage with more than just a narrow task list defined by key performance indicators," adds Arthur.

It's another marker of a trend we are seeing among Open Businesses to move away from spreadsheets – because spreadsheets fail to describe human behavior very well and human behavior is the core bit of what makes any business function.

Transparent businesses need to make their decisions in the open and need to be able to justify them openly. But that does not have to mean "one member, one vote."

"Everyone at Paperight is encouraged to and is supposed to contribute to decision-making. But you can't over do that and become inefficient as a result.

"We don't want to be democratic for democracy's sake, we want to be democratic for effectiveness's sake. I suspect that Open Businesses require an element of benevolent dictatorship from time to time.

"In a closed company people can make decisions on opaque policies without giving real explanations for their decisions, and therefore fewer people take real responsibility.

"In a company that's transparent, someone has to openly say, 'Right, I'll make this decision – and this is why I'm making this call. I'll stand by it – let's go'," Arthur says.

There are limitations on transparency. While Arthur is prepared to share how much profit he can make on each transaction (if a publisher charges a $5 license fee, he'll make 20% of that – $1), he's less inclined to share details about the general finances of the business.

And there's a good reason. In doing so he would risk making transparent other people's business – which he can't claim a right to do.

"You have to be careful about whether you are disclosing your own information or whether or not you are disclosing someone else's information, which they may not be comfortable with," he says.

"That's where we draw the line at the moment – is saying X giving away information that isn't ours to give away."

So is it important to only work with others who also seek to be transparent? Can you infect other less-than-transparent businesses by working with them? Can you be truly transparent when everyone around you is refusing to be?

"We are starting to work with some very big corporate publishers and we have to live with the fact that some are very non-transparent, very opaque. I'm not sure Paperight can teach them much yet, but an organization such as Sourcemap could."

Sourcemap (an MIT-incubated start-up) is a crowd-sourced directory of supply chains founded on the ideal that people have a right to know where products come from, what they are made of, and how they impact both people and the environment.

Its intent, according to founder and CEO Dr Leonardo Bonanni, is that one day soon you'll be able to scan a product on a shelf and find out who made it.

Companies are now coming to Sourcemap and asking for help because supply chains – or more correctly webs – have become so complex they often don't know the roots of their own. In cases like these that becomes paid work on behalf of the corporate concerned. This analysis sometimes involves thousands and thousands of nodes in a supply web.

"Because the companies had paid, they would want to keep the information to themselves, to keep it confidential," says Arthur.

"What's started happening over the last couple of years, according to what I have been told by Dr Bonanni, is that companies have started realizing there would be value in knowing what other people's supply chains were and that would be so valuable that they would be willing to share their own supply chains." he reports.

Necessity is the mother of transparency, it would seem.

That has resulted in either data being shared between clients or, in some cases, being opened up entirely so that we can all understand our industries better.

"In that case the Open-ness did become infectious," says Arthur.

"I would hope the same thing will happen with Paperight."

With Walmart – and the example of Tesco PLC in the introduction to this book – It seems the really big players are moving to a transparency model.

Arthur suggests that this may be a case of being able to become transparent once you have your house in order and you are performing well.

"To some extent you become transparent because you are proud of what you do," he reasons.

Those who aren't in such good shape can't afford to be transparent. And as customers become more and more used to transparency as the new normal they will very quickly start to take opacity to mean you have something to hide.

It will become the badge of the business to avoid.

And that will carry a very high cost indeed.

So. How do you avoid that?

Arthur suggests you must start inside.

"It's very difficult to start being transparent with your external relationships until you start building it into the DNA of your business," he argues.

"The place I feel it would have helped me the most, in my corporate experience, is around functional authority. Make your people the boss of what they do.

"It may not sound directly related to transparency but if you give someone functional authority – let's say you are a machine minder in a printing business and normally you come to work and your job is to make sure the machine runs well and you've got a boss telling you what to do to make sure the machine runs well …

"If instead you say to that person: 'this machine is yours to run – you work out how to make sure it runs at its best', in giving them this area of functional authority, first of all you make them more interested in their job and more curious about how what they do fits into the business. That in turn will trigger you, as a decision-maker, and them to start to share more information about the business.

"You start creating a genuine support base for transparency within the organization itself."

* * *

For Fairphone transparency is a mission. One that ultimately delivers world peace when it is applied to supply chains.

CEO Bas van Abel (formerly the creative director at not-for-profit social innovator Waag Society) is aware that is one hell of a huge ambition for one small social enterprise to achieve, hence the selection of the making of a smartphone to make it tangible.

As the Fairphone website puts it: "You can change the way products are made, starting with a single phone. Together we are opening up the supply chain and redefining the economy, one step at a time."

Fairphone is being as transparent as possible about everything it does; from listing every supplier, to providing a complete break-down of the costs so buyers know exactly where their money is going.

This strong sense of Purpose, combined with the Open-by-default transparency has attracted a community of supporters. Not only did they contribute to design and specification, they now provide invaluable business advice to a small company tackling the complexities of international supply chains.

And when Fairphone called for crowd-funding in order to put the smartphone into production, they raised 4m euros in a month.

"It is much more a philosophy or vision we have than just making a phone. The phone is an artifact to create systemic change," Bas told me.

"At my previous job at Waag Society I was always trying to apply technology in a meaningful way within society. It means working on Open Data, Open Source software, Creative Commons, and, myself a lot on Open Design and Innovation," Bas explains.

One expression of this was his use of Fab Labs – Fabrication Laboratories all around the world that started out with MIT.

The labs use 3D printers and digitally automated milling to distribute production to the point of need. Together with a team, Bas used the techniques in Indonesia to deliver prosthetics made locally for only $50 rather than importing similar items costing tens of thousands of dollars.

"It's all about grass-roots innovation and sharing, and in order to share you need transparency," says Bas.

But even Fairphone, on its mission to change the world, places limitations on transparency. Bas argues that if your every move is observed you become risk averse – and taking risks is important for innovation.

"You might not do things that, in the opinion of a layman, might look weird. So, transparency is a dangerous thing as well."

But, he adds: "Transparency is good for taking responsibility – and being able to take responsibility – to create relationships with the world around you."

You can't form those relationships with the wider world if you do not know, or choose not to know, the impact of what you do upon it. In a state of ignorance – where transparency does not apply – it is possible for designers to send a file across the world and get a product delivered in return – without taking any responsibility for how the raw materials or the labor involved are acquired or treated.

Bas – who expands on his thinking in his co-authored book *Open Design Now* (BIS Publishers 2011) – fears large companies slip into closed thinking as a result of their supply chains. The more you focus on cost efficiency, the more you are likely to end up seeking the most exploitative suppliers. And if, as a result, you cannot be proud of what you do then you are not going to be a fan of the transparent approach.

"We want to create systemic change in the supply chain. Many people already know how the supply chain works in clothing," says Bas.

We have seen results such as the fire that killed hundreds in a factory in Dhaka, Bangladesh, because of unsafe working conditions in May 2013.

"In smartphones it's even worse. People have no idea. Starting with the Congo, four or five million people have died in the last 15 years in conflicts related to mining for your mobile phones," says Bas.

Fairphone is Transparent (Open) by default. That was tough when it meant going to factories in China and insisting their potential production partners supply lists of all their suppliers even before Fairphone could hand over a single penny.

"It took Apple 10 years to publish a list of suppliers for all their products – but you still don't know which one does what.

"We are driven by opening up. If that's the first thing you aim at some companies will shy away, others will embrace it," says Bas.

Transparency is therefore operating as a self-selecting filter for the companies Fairphone could and should be working with.

Fairphone is probably the smallest phone manufacturer in the world. It is operating in a world alongside some of the largest multinationals. That inevitably leads to compromise.

"I hope to be able to show these compromises, in our blogs, etc. There is still child labor in our supply chain. We know that. We can't change everything in one go."

Fairphone's impact goes beyond its own activity.

"Our strategy is also to help people in big companies make changes from within. Our transparency shows we are different, and that allows big companies to treat us differently and be more open to us – we are a movement, not a phone."

Fairphone started as a campaign, became a not-for-profit, and ended up as a company.

How can larger organizations benefit from the value that transparency has offered Fairphone?

Bas thinks it is very hard. His best suggestion is to consider backing a series of start-ups – which operate with transparency in their DNA. Learn from your involvement with them and take back what you learn into your own organization.

"Put the ambitions you can't make happen in your own company in these start-ups.

"I've got CEOs of huge companies advising me on how to do stuff. They know a lot about how to be disruptive but they just can't practice it in their own companies. They use me to do the fun stuff and I give them the platform to do that," says Bas.

Learn through doing – even if it is by doing it with someone else's start-up, he says.

Summary

Transparency is about making your decisions openly, being honest about the criteria on which they are based, and being able to stand by those decisions because of that.

G O A L   S T A T E / W O R S T   C A S E

Where does your business stand from 1 to 5?

Goal state (*scores 5/5*)

Decision-making is done openly, with the process exposed to all employees, stakeholders, and anyone wishing to hold the organization to account. Board meetings (within legal constraints) are open to all and offered as a webcast/webinar.

Worst case (*scores 1/5*)

Decisions are made behind closed doors without explanation. Records are shared only as required by law.

First **steps** …

If you estimate your organization is poor at this start by:

1. Being proud of what you do. If you can't be then transparency is never likely to be good for you. Fix that first.

2. If you are proud of what you do and you want to ramp up the transparency, start by making people the boss of what they do (simplify job descriptions if necessary to define by functional responsibilities).

3. When they start demanding more information about the business to enable them to be that boss, and you start responding with honesty, you are creating the base on which more transparency can be built.

9

Member Led/Customer Led

Definition

Your organization is structured around the formal co-operation of employees, customers, and partners for their mutual social, economic, and cultural benefit.

Everyone wants to be customer-centric. We've never met a board which doesn't harbor that ambition (or one that doesn't want to be innovative for that matter). But being customer-centric is only a step on the journey to being an Open Business.

Most would agree it should be a given. But as customers we find daily evidence, in our interactions with organizations large and small, that it clearly isn't.

Despite the customer-centric intent, tactical thinking often derails the ambition. Managers first think "What's in it for us?" "How can we exploit this data?"

And that shows in their interactions with us time and time again.

Of course they should be thinking "What's in it for our customers?" Identifying what's good for the customer is the best first step to success for the business in any event.

But being customer-centric, laudable as it is, still means you are trying to do something *to* customers.

Being "member led" means you have to think about your relationship with the consumer in a very different way. Instantly the focus is pointed toward partnership. If your customer is your partner, now you want to do things with them rather than do things to them.

do things with the customer rather than to them

Being led by your customers may sound a little radical but it's nothing more than the co-operative movement has been seeking to deliver for more than 200 years.

As a member of a co-operative you have some level of ownership of the organization. Typically – and in the case of the Anglia Regional Co-operative Society (ARCS), headquartered in Peterborough in the UK – it doesn't matter how much you own, you still get one vote. Anyone can stand and be elected to the board, which has executive powers over key business decisions in a business which employs around 1800 people and which operates 27 retail units, 24 funeral homes, 15 travel branches, three opticians, a hair salon, and two department stores.

John Chillcott is CEO at ARCS. He has a background in traditional retail and is long committed to the co-operative cause. He has charged his grocery-funerals-travel-petrol stations business with taking a leading role in developing the co-operative economy in the region in which it operates (essentially East Anglia).

"Your members are your customers. We want them to make a difference in everything from what the retail offering is (is it right? could it be better? how could we involve them in that?); all the way through to how the organization actually operates; the democratic process of engagement through the board, through regional committees.

"We are looking at processes where we could – for example – get a local committee for each store of customers/members to feed up into that process. Some bigger co-ops already have that in place.

"Ultimately we want to make a difference to the community in which we trade. That can mean getting the members to engage with 'what do you do with the profit?'

"The big challenge is lubricating that process."

ARCS has 200,000 members. Not enough of them currently engage.

John wants to find the processes which best take advantage of the very real desire of communities to engage in the organizations that matter to them. A local retail store can be one.

For John, that has meant picking one town as a test bed. It's the relatively prosperous small market town of Halesworth in Suffolk, England.

"There are four-to-six projects going on there now where the local community are very pleased with what we are doing, inviting us on to their various committees.

"There is really good engagement going on. We are sponsoring the community bus, but it's not just a case of sticking our logo on, we serve on the organizing committee, and so on.

"They are now looking at opening a new middle school and looking at making that a co-operative school.

"There's lots you can do when you start to engage with one town. The difficulty is when you have 100 retail units, trying to make that work at scale."

John acknowledges the solution may lay in some of the newer communication techniques available through the web today. He is exploring how straightforward surveys of members can help build the sense of ownership members should have, and how relevant relationships and data from social media can open the committee-democracy of co-operatives to more of their members.

Few would argue that money spent to know the views of your customers is wasted. But what is the return for (in the words of the old co-op ads) being caring and sharing?

The output is trust, naturally. But can we put something tangible against that? In short – what is the business upside of being member led?

Given the interconnectedness of the networked world and the way that enables us to find others to work with on common goals, a co-operative model vs a command and control model seems to make basic common sense. It's a better fit with emerging community values the web brings us. It creates a shared sense of ownership and responsibility – of belonging.

In establishing customers as equal stakeholders (one member one vote, let's not forget) it provides a reason to continue a relationship of trust in a world where loyalty to and trust in large organizations and brands is under constant downward pressure. If you feel you can influence, you feel valued. We see this in brands turning to online influencers to help them co-create outputs. A co-operative offers the opportunity to co-create the business.

if you feel you can influence, you feel valued

In tough times it removes the tension between employee and employer. If you are a member of the organization, if you are part of making the decisions that impact it, you are more highly motivated – more readily accepting.

As John points out, retailer John Lewis Group – which follows many co-operative principles in the way it operates with its staff at least – has been one of the strongest success stories of the triple dip recession that the UK and much of the world has struggled through in the last five years.

Ed Mayo, secretary general, Co-operatives UK said, "In a tough economy, mass ownership is a perfect business strategy because you have your customers and workers onside. The idea of sharing profits with those who are involved in the business is now widely recognized, (but) few companies do it as well as the co-operative sector."

In January 2012, Co-operatives UK published a report which showed four years of growth in the UK's co-operative economy (turning over £35.6bn), outperforming the UK's GDP over the same period by 21%.

Around one billion people are members of co-operatives around the world.

In the case of the Halesworth experiment, John believes the benefits are becoming clear on the ground.

Britain's biggest supermarket chain Tesco owns land right next to the Co-operative food store in Halesworth.

As the sole large retailer in town, the Co-operative may have expected local support for increased competition when Tesco applied to build a store on their land.

But when it came to the crunch the local community – many of whom are members of ARCS – kicked hard against it.

"The great and the good of Halesworth joined with us, sought our advice, and fought off the Tesco proposal.

"It's one of the few towns in the country where being The Co-op has made the difference. Had we been a Sainsburys I don't think there would have been too much objection to Tesco coming along. It would have just been viewed as two corporates fighting it out: Big deal – not our problem.

"The Co-op being challenged by Tesco was regarded as a community issue.

"They felt a genuine sense of engagement – if not yet ownership."

The result was Tesco did not get permission to build and the Co-operative remains the only large grocery retailer in town. Being member led has therefore maintained its market share through creating an army of motivated advocates.

Examples like this may explain why Tesco too is turning to Open Business to rebuild its connection to its customers.

But the bottom line is not the only measure that is important to the organization. If you want people to join with you on a shared journey you had best be able to show them you aren't making the journey at the cost of the world that surrounds them or which will surround their children.

Being member led forces you to operate as if you know the world exists (also a benefit of Open Capital as referenced in that chapter).

John says: "We are now implementing social impact measures. As a co-operative you have to lead with your heart. You can't expect those kinds of measures to have an impact on bottom line in the local store in the near term. It's a 5–10-year engagement and loyalty process."

His co-op is on a journey. And it's not winning every time. When a similar scenario played out in nearby Ramsey, Cambridgeshire, the local people saw the offer of a "planning gain" in a community center offered as a sweetener by the corporate invader (Tesco once again) and took the carrot. John believes there were socioeconomic factors at play.

"In tough economic times, in the case of Ramsey, the chance of a Tesco, with a stronger value proposition, swayed them."

The Co-op has not always been the financial underdog, hoping for community support to defend against new challengers. In the 1970s the Co-op had the same share of market as Tesco enjoys in the UK today. In many ways the Co-op offered a post-war promise to match that of the National Health Service – cradle to grave. Co-ops ran dance halls, and sports and social clubs, delivered milk, and more besides, alongside the functions it remains best known for today – retail, finance, and funerals.

Today's co-operatives dial up the ethical retailing message that has in fact always been at their heart.

"It's why co-ops were invented, to make sure unadulterated goods could be sold to the public at fair prices," said John.

Given the succession of adulterated meat scandals that rocked British grocers in 2013, it's clear there remains high value in the transparency that the close scrutiny of corporate decisions by customers can offer, if only in rebuilding trust.

"130 years on, commercial drive created the same problem – lack of concern for the customer," he says.

Involving customers in key supply chain decisions can make a better business, John believes. But there are challenges. The first is how can you vertically integrate the company to be co-operative top to bottom?

"Stationery suppliers, marketers, printers, food manufacturers, processors, there are co-operatives in all of those sectors – and yet we don't always use them," he said.

"We are co-operative, front-facing, but behind the scenes we are still 'Who's the cheapest?'"

It's an essential step to take when we consider the backdrop of many corporates stepping into this space. They present ever-improving ethical faces. Making "member led" run through the organization, top to bottom, means the beauty of doing the right thing is more than skin deep. And people are very good at seeing past a facade – particularly in our connected world where everyone can publish what they learn through social media.

If you are member led on the surface, but using sweatshop suppliers, don't expect to get away with it for long.

"Since the 1990s we have been businesses that happen to be co-ops, not co-operative businesses. So they haven't vertically integrated with their staff, their suppliers."

The argument then is perhaps to become member led, you have to start by putting your own house in order.

Currently it is very hard for the average membership card-carrying co-op customer to realize what their ownership means. For many they would not be able to describe it in terms which were any different from any other corporate's loyalty card.

"They used to be able to – when it was a share dividend you got," says John.

"If you didn't redeem or spend your dividend throughout the year it built up in your share account – which effectively was your ownership stake in the business. No matter how much was in there, you didn't get any more say – it's always been one member one vote.

"But you had capital invested in the business. What people probably never realised was that this was risk capital – they regarded it as a kind of deposit, but it is an investment in the business. Co-ops have shied away from that, because of the grey area between risk and deposit capital. We haven't done much share capital raising as a result so it remains an avenue with huge potential if we can get the business successful enough that people feel they want to invest in it."

John's thinking is coinciding with the Open Capital opportunities for crowd-funding we examined in Chapter 2.

"I could absolutely see a crowd-funding platform to be used to launch a new store," he says.

John thinks the success of such a project would depend on the social capital existing in the community. The potential for tapping into that is huge. After only a few months of focused effort in Halesworth the community turned to the co-operative for support and inspiration when planning a new school.

"They are looking at a co-operative school so we have got the Co-operative Schools Trust involved. We're funding the revamp of a community center. In poorer communities it is there, but it's harder to tap into.

"And that's where a true sense of ownership, a true sense of being led by our members becomes so important."

Already 50% of ARCS shoppers are members. In terms of the spend they represent, it is nearer 70%.

"I don't think we've done enough yet to make them feel a part of the business – able to change things, make things happen, improve the offer," he admits.

At Halesworth the approach is starting to bear fruit. Complaints are down, profits are up. There are a number of metrics to suggest they are doing the right thing. But not enough yet to put a number against every action, John explains.

His advice for those planning to take the Member Led route is to plan for the long, but worthwhile, run.

"Securing a place, as a business, as trusted in the community, has got to be a win."

The process for gathering member views to lead the business is currently relatively ad hoc and traditional. Captured word of mouth in stores is fed back to the center.

John sees new technologies allowing that to scale and accelerate. And the first focus will be on the offer in the store – and what customers would like to see.

"Social media, modern communications – they open all this up for us. But there's a lot of inertia to overcome. In traditional hierarchical structures managers feel threatened by engagement with their customers, believe it or not."

It's part of the legacy of command and control. Managers brought up within the old model have been rewarded and recognized for their decision-making and leadership. In member-led models we are asking them to share the decision making power, and lead in a far less directive style.

we are asking them to share the decision-making power

Importantly for the embedding of a shift from center-out command and control, to edge-in member led, ARCS has already stopped most of its broadcast-style advertising. Leaflet blasts to 200,000 people, newspaper adverts, it's all been stopped.

That's been replaced by a more focused targeting of members, and specific groups of members.

Another area for reform is the role of the store manager.

"Really, replenishment and stock control is so automated now, you could have the situation where a store manager becomes much more an overseer of the store's relationship with the community.

"That's a very different type of manager, with very different skills."

John has arrived at this view after what he regards as two failed experiments in running "member engagement" as a separate function in the business.

"When it operates as a silo – 'Hey Mr Manager, you look after your store, and we'll look after your members' – it doesn't work. There are too many head-to-heads going on at all levels of the business with that."

Instead the thinking must be embedded throughout. If the organization is member led then of course finding ways for members to engage becomes essential for everyone in the company.

And crucially it must start with the primary interface with members – which remains the store.

That's going to mean the re-writing of store manager job descriptions – but also of job descriptions throughout the organization. If you set out that you are led by your members as a primary principle then that should inform how staff are measured and rewarded. Success criteria shift.

For store managers John sees the new prime objectives as being: "To establish your store within your community, engage with your owners (your members) to create an offer and experience that works in that town for those people."

This runs counter to what was thought was the right idea in the 1990s, which was to centralize buying, have a standard range, have each store offering the same promotions, prices, and ranges.

John says: "You then try to get clever with automated regionalization. But I don't think automation can ever get down to really knowing the needs of a specific town or village."

"We have to find a way to put that local power back into the store – into the hands of the people who run it and the members who shop in it."

This is a throwback in many ways to the autonomy store managers enjoyed in the 1980s. But instead of teams of skilled buyers and a manager's gut instinct, with more and more ways to gather the data needed, faster and locally, there may not be the need to rebuild layers of localized costs – instead relying on the lead supplied by members.

Today that means John believes a co-op store is there to provide goods and services to meet community needs of an assured quality, but also to use the fruits of that trade to benefit the community in which it operates.

Fundamentally this is a shift from center to edge – the kind of shift the web seems to drive. Just as control, production, and consumption of media has moved in large part into the hands of individuals and away from large centralized organizations, is this same democratization something that can be applied to the companies which seek to serve our needs?

While John and many CEOs like him are happy to allow customers to lead on decisions which have a direct impact on their daily experience (e.g., "What should we stock to meet your needs, what should the experience be in the store?") where else can he see an advantage to opening up to customer-led decision-making.

   "Social and environment impact are good examples: What should we be doing about our carbon footprint or ethical buying? What should we be doing about our vehicle fleet? What should our remuneration policy be, what should the ratio of pay between the CEO and a checkout operator be?

   "These are the kind of things you would want members to have a say on. At the moment to have a say you have to be on the board."

And that's a problem. Anyone can be on the board, but that means you can come to the decision-making body with inadequate experience – and potentially with an agenda which is against the wider interests of the organization.

Some larger co-ops invest in a staircase of steps to that decision-making board. They have local and regional boards and sub-boards which people can progress through.

That means the whole body of members can only vote on who gets onto the lowest step of the staircase. Who progresses to the higher levels of the hierarchy is selected by the committees and sub-boards.

"Is that right? It ensures you don't get anarchy in the boardroom. Co-ops nearly got wiped out in the 90s precisely because of their vulnerability to their own democratic structure."

Manchester-born entrepreneur and polar explorer Andy Regan attempted a hostile takeover in 1997.

One of the routes Regan attempted was to flood decision-making bodies with his supporters. (It was an extremely messy affair which it is not the role of this book to rake over. The Wikipedia article on Andrew Regan contains all the links should you choose to investigate for yourself.)

For our purposes what Regan's attempt did do is reveal the risk of being open to customer leadership on every decision.

His offer to members was effectively: vote for my people to get on boards, we'll demutualize – and you will all get £1000.

Which raises the question of value to members. While it's easy to reel off the advantages to the organization of becoming increasingly member led (more complete customer knowledge, making better fit products and services, creating advocates, reducing marketing spend, etc.) how much does the customer value this approach?

In 1990s Britain £1000 was the price they put on it.

But let's go back to Halesworth in 2013. The community has resisted bringing competition into the town to protect the local businesses (not just the Co-op) they feel engaged with, and they are prepared to pay a premium for that.

That's quite a commitment. And that's after just a handful of projects extending the role of the local store in the community. How much trust do you have to place in a business before handing it an influential role in the education of your children? In turning to the local co-op for support with plans for a co-operative middle school the people of Halesworth have already shown they score the value of the relationship way beyond that £1000 benchmark of 1990s Britain.

How much more could they value their ownership of the business in the years to come as John's vision to make his co-operative society more member led comes to fruition?

"Democracy has its perils for commercial decision-making," says John, "but there are plenty of opportunities through new channels, through new media, which means people can be influential rather than directional."

New technologies also offer the opportunity to solve the issue of scale – of ensuring the views of more than the handful of members who make it to the decision-making boards have a role in leading decision-making.

"Understanding and measuring influence, what vibes we are getting, and how that should shape our policies and what we do, can help us improve this," said John.

Through the monitoring of relevant conversation – online or off – we lower the barrier for people to tell us what they think. Where once they would have to visit in person, or write a letter, now they can email or comment on our official websites or social properties (Facebook, Twitter, etc.) More often still, they just tell each other. Listening out for those conversations about you but not directed at you can be even more critical and more valuable than the two-way directly between you and the customer (as we will discover in the next chapter, on Trust).

And of course the solution to "taking the temperature" of your customers need not be left in the online realm. At London Heathrow's Terminal 5 – and increasingly elsewhere – you'll find a simple series of red/amber/green buttons to punch to rate your experience that day.

Waitrose issues you with a green token at the checkout with which you are encouraged to "vote" by dropping them into one of three containers to express your support for which local charity Waitrose should make its next donation to.

Online activity scales this but shouldn't replace it. It can be simple.

John believes the key question an organization must ask itself to become member led is: "What can I do for our customer?" But the rules surrounding most make that difficult – since they must put the needs of shareholders first.

"How do you take the wind out of the shareholders' sails and give a bit more power to the customers and the people who work in the organization? In a co-op the shareholders and the members are one and the same."

For private and smaller businesses the first step is easier, John says.

"Start your democracy inside – with your employees."

Staff at ARCS are now auto-enrolled as members. They have to actively take a decision to opt-out. Only about 1% do opt-out. That means that everything that members get, employees get. That includes communications.

"We're also giving employee-members a bonus dividend level," said John.

"We don't want to create too much of a two-tier thing but if you can make your employees feel they are special members – and therefore advocates of the business – then I think that's a powerful message."

John's ambition is now to take his Anglia Regional Co-op and make it a model of how co-operatives ought to be in the 21st century – presenting a lesson to other larger co-operatives.

While he's at it he's giving a great steer to anyone who is ready to make customers their partners, to become more member or customer led.

* * *

For most NASDAQ-listed companies with revenues of around $7bn, becoming a co-operative is not really an option, and for the most part, not on the agenda. But that does not mean they can't be customer led. Indeed vehicle hire multinational Avis Budget Group lives by the mantra "Customer Led, Service Driven."

For Larry De Shon, president of Avis Budget EMEA, that means listening and responding to customer need in order to help customers better live their lives.

At time of writing Larry was in the midst of a massive program of transformation to integrate 12 national Avis and Budget businesses across EMEA. The multimillion-euro-a-year investment project carries at its heart a strategy to give customer-facing staff more time to actually be face-to-face with customers.

Those things that distract a front desk employee from dealing with the person in front of them are being stripped out, reorganized, or relocated. For example, an international multicultural and multilingual hub in Barcelona now takes calls for bookings and offers customer support during the period of your car rental. Another in Budapest deals with post-hire customer service issues (among other business support functions). Digital marketing is being centralized in Bracknell, UK (Larry's EMEA-wide HQ).

"The real value is out there with the customers and in understanding what it is they want from us. We want our country management teams to focus as much time as possible on this," says Larry.

And for those customers who want speed and convenience over human interaction, the organization must respond with the digital technologies they demand, he says.

That's leading to completely new websites for both Avis and Budget in EMEA, which were due to go live in 2014.

"We didn't want to just do a better car rental site. We are trying to build a site where customers can quickly get what they need – and just what they need," says Larry.

This is a critical factor in being customer led. A company which keeps offering you things you don't need is less likely to be seen as anything other than trying to make a fast buck from you. You are much more likely to believe a company has your interests at heart when it has listened carefully to what you need and then done its best to provide the best-fit solution.

If I tell you I am traveling alone on business and you try to up-sell me a child seat I'm not likely to think well of you. In the case of the new websites for EMEA, that means asking questions to identify the customers' real needs up front. Then it will deliver transparently priced, WYSIWYG packages.

Social media has found a new role in the business with nine new hires in 2013, eight of whom are focused on listening direct to the needs of customers from an international hub in Barcelona.

"I am so pleased with how the social media strategy is coming together," says Larry.

The international team uses social media monitoring technology to "listen" to openly published conversations in seven languages.

Their focus is on direct sales – finding people expressing real-time need for Avis or Budget services and meeting those needs.

"We have a great, passionate team and watching them jumping into conversations and helping with customer needs is a real inspiration," says Larry.

The concept places the Avis Budget Group brands right at the front of the customer's mind at just the moment they are making their decision.

The team's online monitoring means it can also offer a supporting role in identifying and accelerating customer service issues.

Crucially for the customer led agenda, the data they gather from online conversations can also be analyzed for insight and distributed to departments across the business to bring them ever closer to real-time customer need.

"I think this part of the company will get bigger and bigger and useful to more and more people," says Larry.

Being customer led also demands a renewed focus on clarity, and that too results in ever-closer working relationships with customers.

Larry explains that Gina Bruzzichesi, senior vice president, Strategic Customer Leadership in the US, has been responsible for a huge tranche of work to evaluate communications from the company at every customer touch point.

Her role – which she took up in 2010 – is essentially to be the customer advocate in the organization.

Gina (a lawyer by training) and her team went through everything from rental agreements to the letters an insurance adjuster might send you when settling a claim. They re-wrote everything to make it more customer-friendly – ripping out the acronyms and legalese wherever possible and demystifying T&Cs. And in most cases they did this hand-in-hand with customers – co-creating an output to suit the needs of real people.

But that is just one sign of the significant cultural change the customer led agenda is requiring of Avis Budget Group.

Like so many examples we have shared, it was an agenda born from crisis – the economic crisis of 2008.

"At that time (November 21, 2008) our stock went down to 38 cents," said Gina – not much more than one hundredth of its value in summer 2013.

"We survived through what many thought would destroy us as a company. As a result of coming out of that our CEO (and chairman, Ron L Nelson) did a lot of reflection and basically said that the time at which the industry builds itself back up is the time at which we had to differentiate ourselves," said Gina.

The cars are the commodity – the service and the experience was where Avis Budget Group could make a difference.

"What I realized was that it wasn't just a matter of distinguishing ourselves in the industry, but of making the brand one which transcends our industry and is known everywhere for delivering great customer service," said Gina.

If you are familiar with the story of shoe (and clothes) retailer Zappos you will note similarities.

"Zappos is a customer service company that just happens to sell shoes," as CEO Tony Hsieh famously put it in his first book *Delivering Happiness* (Business Plus 2010). It's no surprise to discover Gina spent time at Zappos, taking inspiration. It was one of 50 best-in-class companies she investigated.

What she also took from her learning was that Avis Budget Group should allow customers to prioritize its investments. And that the key to success is the culture of the business.

She therefore arrived at a road map which focused on three core capabilities:

- Knowing your customers: What will keep them coming back as well as what will drive them away?
- To use that knowledge to personalize the experience for them. It doesn't have to be perfect, but it does have to feel personal, says Gina. "As much as you need technology and innovation to help meet customer expectation, you also need to make sure there is an emotional connection, and that is always going to be made through people."
- The third core capability therefore is engagement of your people. "We call it acting with engagement," she says.

With the roadmap in place, the intervening years have seen a range of initiatives and programs which have all been about embedding the culture.

"This is where we've seen a huge change and improvement. People feel pride about the brand and the company they work for, they feel good about coming to work, they feel engaged, giving us their discretionary effort," she said of Avis Budget Group in 2013.

One very significant way in which the customer experience has been supported is by giving ownership of it to every member of staff. They are all now empowered to resolve customer issues. It means everyone is in customer service in the business. When you make improving the lives of your customers everyone's concern it is much easier to become led by their needs.

everyone is in customer service in the business

Staff now get a Customer Service Resolution Toolkit.

"It means you as an employee, no matter whether you park the cars or serve behind the counter, are empowered to resolve customer service issues with a range of options – starting with an apology and working up to reimbursement in some way."

"And it's working. We had record-breaking (2012) employee survey scores and record-breaking Voice of the Customer scores," said Gina.

The Voice of the Customer scores (based on rapid follow-up with customers about their recent experiences) are on the agenda at every senior team meeting and everyone in the business is now familiar with them and their importance – such is the focus on the customer.

"What we have done really well is the culture piece. Our next focus must be on knowing our customers better and being able to personalize the experience in an optimum way," she says.

What Gina is also now keen to understand is the impact on loyalty (and therefore lifetime customer value) from the investments made so far – and from potential future investments in the Customer Led agenda.

That agenda is due an EMEA-wide relaunch in 2014 and EMEA President Larry De Shon is open to scaling some of the co-creation process the US started on, through open iterations in social media.

Cutting the time it takes to hear what customers are saying about their experience with you offers significant wins, too, says Larry.

In earlier versions of the "Voice of the Customer" reports that Airport Rental Station managers receive (based on responses to after-hire emails) there was a 90-day delay. By the time they hit the managers' inboxes, the customers making complaints had usually given up and written off Avis Budget Group as unresponsive. It is hard to be led by events happening in your rearview mirror.

Today managers get real-time reports, along with a suite of tools to measure the effectiveness of changes they make in response to complaints or other issues raised, says Larry.

Managers (in the US) are now connected in a forum for shared best practice. So if they are stuck for ideas in response to the live feedback they are getting, there is a wealth of support available from peers to create an effective plan of action.

The method has proved to be a powerful driver of loyalty: Managers are expected to make personal calls to customers who have important concerns.

Despite initial dread, says Larry, more often than not the managers get positive feedback from their customers for doing so. And the customers feel a renewed connection to the brand.

Adding social media monitoring data to the emails they are already gathering may follow in due course, to give managers an even more complete picture of their performance from the customers' point of view – and the opportunity to scale that loyalty.

The more customers lead, the better fit with their need you can expect to deliver – building both loyalty and affinity.

And no matter what kind of business or organization you are operating in, there is room to start shifting the relationship you have with customers from one in which you do something to them toward one in which you do something with them.

Summary

The most directional of all the principles, being member or customer led means doing things *with* your customers and staff rather than *to* them. It means you strive to treat them as genuine partners.

GOAL STATE / WORST CASE

Where does your business stand from 1 to 5?

Goal state (*scores 5/5*)

100% of all key decisions (within legal constraints) are made by and with those charged with implementing them in collaboration with partner-customers (members) and/or wider supporters of the organization.

Worst case (*scores 1/5*)

All key decisions are made at board level and imposed downwards on those charged with implementing them. Stakeholders and customers are considered only in the context of what can be gained from them.

First **steps** ...

If you estimate your organization is poor at this start by:

1. Listing how a partner in the business should expect to be treated. How well does that map against how you regard your customers?

2. Testing democracy inside – with your staff. Trial simple voting mechanisms to gauge opinion on issues that are important to them. For example, where should the Christmas party be held this year? What should be on the menu in the staff canteen? Report back on the opinions and the outcomes.

3. Build on those first tests by defining areas where you are comfortable testing further democratic leadership by staff. Discover the limitations which should apply in your organization and think about what safeguards and controls will be appropriate.

chapter **10**

Trust

 (decorative chapter heading)

Definition

Mutually assured reliance on the character, ability, strength, or truth of the partnership.

Activated together, the nine other Principles of Open Business combine to deliver the 10th. Trust is a far from insignificant output of Open Business.

Without trust there can be no relationships of any value. Without relationships there can be no organizations, no customers, no believers, no advocates, no future.

Google Executive Chairman Eric Schmidt went as far as to say in his 2009 University of Pennsylvania Commencement Address that: "In a networked world, trust is the most important currency."

Every politician, every newspaper editor, every CEO, every brand manager, every one of us knows it is essential. It is what ties customers to brands, families to each other, organizations and societies together. It is a very human trait and one which has given us an evolutionary advantage defined at its simplest as: "I'll scratch your back if you'll scratch mine."

Evidence from neuroscience (e.g., "The Neurobiology of Trust" by Paul J Zak in *Scientific American*, 2008) suggests we get chemical feel-good rushes to reward us when we trust and are trusted, and that there are large portions of the brain developed specifically to deal with its complexities. Being able to trust our neighbor allowed us to build civilizations. We've evolved to demand it.

To work closely with people, requires it. Partnership, the paradigm of Open Business, demands it.

And when trust diminishes we are in crisis. We saw in the opening chapters how Tesco PLC identified its trust issue as its burning platform – its catalyst for shifting to Open Business.

That crisis is where so many of today's organizations find themselves. Trust, by almost any measure you care to mention has shifted from the center to the edge: from a faith in government, media, corporation, to a faith in each other, what we say to each other, and our own relationships. We trust government, institutions, and brands less than we did. If the neuroscience is any guide that is because we feel our trust in them has not been reciprocated We trusted them and, in lesson after lesson, they failed to repay that trust.

In an increasingly connected, always-on, everyone-able-to-publish world, transparency becomes a default. More of us are equipped and able to find out more of the things they didn't want us to know about – and to share it with more of us, more swiftly than ever before (media has done well out of this global whistle-blowing, by the way, its score rising on Edelman's Trust Barometer in 2013).

Social media has in part revealed this, in part accelerated it. It has revealed it by showing the interconnectedness of our world like never before. It has accelerated it by enabling us to self-organize at next to no cost and in next to no time. It took away so much of the friction of organization, reducing the transaction cost of making things happen.

Before social media it took time and resource to create a space to invite people into, to find them, to bring them together, and to surface their solutions to shared need. It took the kind of thing we called the means of production. And that was owned by the center.

Today everyone has access to the same organizational infrastructure. For example, after the London riots of the summer of 2011, crowds took to the streets armed with brooms for a mass clear up. This was not organized from the center, but via a Twitter hashtag. It was self-organized by people to whom it mattered. Had the center tried the same it is likely the response would have been considerably weaker. Self-organization breeds self-determination.

self-organization breeds self-determination

According to the annual Edelman Trust Barometer (which has now included more than 30,000 respondents in more than 20 markets) "earned media" was more credible than advertising 10 years ago. In 2005 trust started shifting from "authorities" (the center) to peers (each other). By 2009 trust in business was collapsing, leading Edelman to call on companies to partner with governments in a bid to rebuild it. By 2012 the survey found trust in government was crumbling, too.

To complete the picture there was a slight upturn in most sectors covered by the report in 2013 – which we suggest is more likely to be characteristic of a dead cat bounce than green shoots of recovery.

Where resurgence is stronger and more sustained you will find corporations which have shifted their view of trust: from an economic one (in which reliability of transaction is king) to the more human one demanded of (and delivered by) Open Business.

Trust, for an Open Business, is a measure of the belief in the honesty, fairness, or benevolence of another party. Build this kind of reciprocal trust and your partners are more likely to forgive your failures of competence; they will cut you slack if they trust that you are trying to do your best for them and being honest when things go wrong.

This delivers more resilient and meaningful relationships with stakeholders; builds brand equity – and therefore shareholder value; offers cut-through in cluttered markets (choosing the brand you trust acts as a shortcut for decision-making); creates a very human, emotional connection with customers, partners and employees, reducing the cost of both acquisition and retention.

It is this kind of trust which cannot be built behind closed doors and the kind that has been both required and delivered by taking the Open road at advertising agency Grey London.

You can't radically reshape the way you do business – pushing out responsibility to the people traditionally viewed as at the bottom of the hierarchy – without trust. Open thinking at Grey London placed trust in staff and delivered trust from clients. Both sets of stakeholders bought into the emerging culture to such an extent that results have shown growth in quarter after quarter ever since the project began in 2008.

Before embarking on the journey to Open, the company was struggling, says CEO Chris Hirst. Yes, this is another story of an established business that needed a crisis to reap the rewards of Open. (Hint: You should probably not wait for a crisis.)

"It was basically a dog of a business," says Chris, after we had found our way to one of the few remaining meeting rooms in which to record our interview. "It had to change if it was going to thrive.

"We had a very clear line in the sand, a classic burning platform, and we then went through a classic stepped management change program. It was very deliberately done."

The intent wasn't to become an Open Business. The ambition was to become the kind of creative business other creative businesses aspired to be. Open is where they ended up when they looked for the best answer to meet the needs of the world they found around themselves.

"We started looking at what the culture ought to be, what we wanted it to be if we wanted to be a real world-class creative business in the 21st century. Through an evolutionary process, we came to start to call that culture 'Open'."

Today you are greeted by the words **Open** and **Long** in bold script as you arrive at the offices in London's Hatton Garden: "Open" for the culture, "Long" for the impact of the ideas they seek to create.

Over time Chris came to realize that Grey London's culture was (and is) its strategy.

"If I had to define one thing that we do, it would be culture, and our culture is Open," he says.

"Open grew to encompass everything because all we are is people in a building, so therefore all we are is our culture. I could argue that it's not people that are our most important assets, but our culture. Our people will come and go," says Chris.

all we are is people in a building

Once on its journey the team had to start describing what this "reference point creative business" might look like. They put some numbers behind that. And they published them, on the walls in reception. Ambitions, bold ambitions, were shouted out loud.

"We hit some, and we missed some," Chris admits, "but it focused people's minds and people commented on them when they came in."

What surprised visitors was that an advertising agency would do such a thing because once you set targets publicly, you can publicly fail. That too, is part of being Open – being honest and vulnerable and understanding the consequences of that.

Grey London stated that by 2012 they wanted to be agency of the year. People laughed. Ok, so they didn't hit that high point – but they upset enough applecarts when they landed third spot that year.

People-based businesses (at least those where talent wins you a premium) are simply buildings with people in, Chris argues.

"What that means is that our competitors are just buildings with people in, too. I remember thinking to myself, so why are their 200 people doing so much better than our 200 people. What is the difference?"

Some differences were tangible – ownership structure, history, heritage, the kind of client base they had. But Chris couldn't change any of those in the short term. What he could change was culture.

The first thing to know and to believe, he says, was that huge change is possible. Carlos Ghosn's famous turnaround of Nissan at the turn of the century was one example that inspired Chris. Massive change in a 100,000-person enterprise could be achieved – and fast.

"Be really ambitious about the amount of change that is possible – don't look for incremental change. Be super ambitious," says Chris.

People think of culture as an intangible – something that they can get around to fixing later. Chris thinks culture is a harder, more physical thing.

"To change or sustain it you have to physically do things. That's where people fall down. They list their values in a powerpoint and think 'Job done'.

"We started by describing the kind of environment that we thought we should work in to create change ..." That meant outlining some new behaviors.

Advertising agencies can be very conservative environments in which creative directors sit in corner offices lording it over a hierarchy of dependency, warns Chris.

"They are big groups of highly motivated individuals who, compared to the rest of the population, are very highly paid, highly educated people. What we then do is set about creating an organizational structure which basically squashes all of that with processes and sign-offs. We take all of these brilliant people and put them into a very conventional pyramidal hierarchy.

"The creative director's sign-off is the ultimate expression of that and creates a dependent culture."

Chris turned the pyramid upside down, putting the emphasis on those working face-to-face with his clients.

"We wanted to change our relationship with clients, putting them at the heart of what we do. We realized that if we wanted to change our relationship with clients we had to start by changing the relationships we had with each other."

They set about pulling out of the way all of the things which could prevent client-facing staff from being as good as they could be.

Now Grey London does not have a set agency process. There is no sign-off by the creative director. Teams are built around client problems (rather than the conventional model of squeezing a client's problem into the available team structure). Offices for individuals don't exist (the few rooms with doors that close are in short supply as meeting rooms), people don't sit in departments.

"The beauty of Open is that it's a very simple thing to understand (though more complicated to nurture)."

The actions they took (in removing offices and processes, for example) offered demonstrations of Open in action.

"We set about doing things before we started presenting them. We did focus groups with virtually everybody in the company and got the people in the organization to help us with the actions, with the language, with the expression of what Open could mean.

"This isn't my culture, this is our culture – everyone has to feel like this is something they are part of," he says.

"We didn't invent any of this. We just did it with a degree of single-mindedness and we stuck at it."

One of Chris's favorite quotes comes from US President Ronald Reagan:

"The nine scariest words in the English language are 'I'm from the government and I'm here to help.'"

It reminds him that getting out of the way is critical to the success of Open – and that means you must trust your staff. If you are to rebuild trust there seems no better place to start.

Both staff engagement scores and client satisfaction scores have improved significantly since the Open Culture project began – indicating trust is building.

Other indicators suggest trust is helping build hard business results, too. It has a particular role to play in new business – where clients are signing on the dotted line before having tangible knowledge of what they are going to get.

trust is helping build hard business results

"We've won huge amounts of new business. We are a premium business and we have grown our total client base by at least as much as we have grown organically from our pre-existing clients.

"We are about double the size we were in 2010 with the growth of completely new revenue approximately equal to growth in incremental revenue," says Chris.

Prior to the shift, the trend had been gradually downward.

"You have to say there is an element of trust improvement in this because our existing clients were willing to commit more projects to us than they were previously and the consultants and the brokers in the market who bring clients to us were more happy to do that."

What Grey London has achieved by taking this Open stance is something to believe in – something to which both talent and clients can rally. Continuing to act in an open manner will build trust in the Grey London brand. Each action in line with its cultural ambition reinforces the belief for those within and without.

What is still left to do?

Chris believes he hasn't yet been good enough at "writing it down." He has lots of versions, but wants to keep striving to come up with one to which more behaviors can be attached – demonstrating through doing.

It is still quite hard (perhaps too hard) for a lot of people to accept the power that trust in this flattened hierarchy requires that they exercise. Many – perhaps more used to command and control structures – find themselves struggling to adapt. More work is needed here, Chris concedes.

A new induction process is emerging with a view to going some way toward fixing that.

Some staff may have to learn to trust themselves and trust that the organization will support rather than punish errors made in taking their first leaps.

"Give us 5/10 at the moment – because as a concept Open has so much more to give."

Despite the so-so score Chris is proud of the progress so far. Grey London is owned by WPP – a very large advertising and marketing corporation – bound by all the high levels and complexities of corporate governance you would expect. It's no freewheeling start-up.

"Advertising agencies rail against this kind of thing out of fear of having their creativity constrained. What's interesting about Open for us is that we found very little conflict between us, our desire to change, and those 'corporate constraints.'

"We've done 'Open' within quite a conventional business environment. We didn't get cut any slack – every quarter since we did this we've hit our numbers and our numbers have improved for 16, 17, 18 quarters. There's very few business in the world which are able to say that since 2008."

Acknowledging that Open is the default for early-stage businesses today, he adds: "Open is the way the big guys get to compete with the start-ups."

But no one ever says being Open is easy.

Chris warns: "Very few things are impossible but virtually everything is very, very difficult. In order to get stuff done you have to be prepared to live in the space between very, very difficult and impossible.

"When you realize that, it's quite a liberating thing because. First of all, you stop feeling like a complete failure.

"What do you need to live in that gap? Stamina, energy, courage, will, imagination, and thick skin."

The message is, says Chris, "You can do it – just don't expect it to be easy and don't feel like you are failing because it feels very, very, difficult.

"Just pick somewhere to start. If you really are going to change ask yourself what are you going to do to make sure Monday feels different than Friday did?"

* * *

To have trust you have to believe the other person has your interests at heart – and that's as true for brands and organizations as it is for individuals, argues Ivan Palmer, drawing on 30 years in marketing as a creative director (at Joshua, the UK's first through-the-line agency) and, since 2005, as the founder of The Social Partners – one of the UK's longest established social marketing agencies.

His journey has taught him many lessons about trust.

In pre-Internet economies brands could rely on, build propositions around, and place trust in, a Unique Selling Point. The proposition, the positioning to the buyer, could last 5–10 years – and in some cases even longer, says Ivan.

The Internet meant it was easier to bring copycat propositions or products to market quicker. The innovation advantage was reduced. That meant the cycle of brand reinvention had to become quicker too, plummeting to 6–12 months.

"It became obvious that brand trust is something you need to win constantly, again and again and again," he says.

In the old model you were only as good as your last action. The brand trust relationship was personal. The promises and building of value may be made on a mass level but the moment of truth happened at the individual – in a personal experience.

"That's where the values manifest. At that point I either accept those values, they become cemented, and I trust the brand, or it fell short of those promises, in which case there was no trust," says Ivan.

Now the moment of truth has shifted from your own experience, to that of anyone within your social network.

The consequence, says Ivan, is that brand marketing is now really relationship marketing. It used to be about creating images, values, equity – a world that could be controlled.

brand marketing is now really relationship marketing

"I could craft values, personality: How does this brand behave? What are my beliefs? What do I promise? What is my purpose? That would be delivered through my messaging, and also through my packaging, and anything you would touch as a consumer.

"The interesting thing now is that I can still do all that, but the first moment of truth (or what Google calls the Zero Moment of Truth) is somebody else's experience. Therefore, to build trust the customer experience is now more important and returns better value than delivering messaging and promise," says Ivan.

Look at John Lewis – the UK department store retailer – says Ivan. They spent as much on customer goodwill, on improving the customer experience, and on delivering a reputation for customer-centric service, as most companies would spend on advertising. It has paid dividends for them. Results from 2013 saw them deliver profits of £415m (up 13.8% against a backdrop of general retail gloom) and staff sharing in £210m in bonuses.

"A lot of brands haven't realized yet that you can keep on promising stuff, but the 0.01% of bad experiences completely out-shouts the 99.99% of experiences which do meet the brand promise. Because that's the stuff that surfaces – and where trust is destroyed," he adds.

Ivan's research has uncovered "a clear causality" between trust and purchasing behavior: People who trust brands will pay a premium of 43%, they will stay with the brand longer, and they will buy a wider range of your products and services, he says.

A global survey by WPP and the Futures Company "found that the (most trusted) brand in each of the 22 countries we researched was nearly seven times more likely to be purchased and consumers were 10 times more likely to have formed a strong bond."

Edelman's 2012 Trust Barometer found that if a company lacks trust people are more inclined to believe negative things they hear about it and trade less with them as a result.

Building trust requires a shift in the order of priorities for many businesses. It means placing the good of the customer ahead of profit (and therefore ahead of the – at least direct – good of the shareholder). Profit should be a consequence. It's the KPI of fulfilling your primary objective (delivering the customer agenda).

Ivan's experience in CRM (customer relationship management) provides evidence to support this: 94% of all the initial CRM projects failed in the first two–three years because they started from the proposition: "How Can We Extract More Value From Consumer Relationships?" The 6% that succeeded asked the question: "How Can We Create More Value For Consumers."

"That's the heart of trust: That you believe someone is trying to do good for you," he says.

And, he argues, this presents a challenge for brands.

"Advertising makes you unhappy – it tells you about things you haven't got, to show you the life you aren't leading. The American Dream is the American Nightmare."

The problem for this in the context of trust is that this doesn't appear to be in the best interest of the customer.

"Brands need to find a way for their relationships to have a mutual purpose," says Ivan.

Broadcasting idealized images, isn't the solution, Ivan argues.

"If someone is constantly managing their image, I don't know if I can trust them. I think, 'this is what they want me to think', so I don't tend to trust that kind of person," he adds.

Brands have to re-orient themselves away from mass toward one-to-one relationships in which the individual gets a sense that the brand is working for them, that it has the customer's interest as its core purpose, says Ivan.

How can they do that?

They have to become more nurturing, more enabling, more plural. In Ivan's words, more female.

"The majority of legacy brands are masculine," says Ivan. "They tell you how to live your life. That's a masculine behavior. 'BT: It's Good To Talk.' That tells you how to live.

"A lot of more modern brands ask a question – which is a feminine behavior: Where would you like to go today? What can I do for you? What would you like to create? These are enabling questions. The brand becomes less dominant and more nurturing and supportive, helping you grow – a feminine role.

"The masculine role is assertive, providing, leading. It's where a lot of brands have been. Interestingly for me Open (and social) is much more of a feminine behavior," says Ivan.

Ivan's advice for brands is to place users' needs and interests at the heart of what they do. They have to prove this not through telling people that they have their interests at heart, but by demonstrating it. They have to win trust one customer at a time, one experience at a time. They also have to value the outputs of those experiences.

win trust one customer at a time

The late Randy Pausch – a scientist and professor at Carnegie Mellon – told a great story in his last lecture (*The Last Lecture*, Randy Pausch and Jeffrey Zaslow, Hyperion 2008). When he was 12, he and his sister were treated to a visit to Disney World by their parents. While there, the kids wanted to show mum and dad how grateful they were and chose to buy a ceramic salt and pepper shaker from the Disney gift shop.

As Randy rushed back to his parents to excitedly show them the gift they had chosen, he accidently dropped the shaker – which shattered.

A passing adult suggested they take it back to the store. Not expecting the best of outcomes, young Randy was blown away when he returned the broken shaker to a Disney employee who responded by saying: "Gee, I'm sorry. I didn't wrap that well enough."

The item was replaced at a cost of a couple of bucks. Randy calculated that over the years that small moment of consideration had resulted in him and his family spending a further $100,000 with the Disney brand.

Further, he was retelling that story almost literally to his dying day – all around the world. And right there, is how it scales. In an era of social media, in an era of our Zero Moment of Truth being someone else's experience, the impact of that one story is huge and headed straight for your bottom line.

"Only five people may hear of that story in a week. But over time that story gets told and retold. The value of that personal story outweighs the glossy ad with the celebrity endorsement because this is where trust is built – not in your messaging, but in your behavior," says Ivan.

It seems you can't broadcast trust.

"Large-scale brands must shift their heads away from a broadcast reach perspective and think, 'if I can create 100 of those stories a week it's going to out-weigh the $1m I spend a week on placed advertising which makes a claim about what we do and what we don't do.'

"That's why, whether or not they realize it yet, brands are in an era of relationship marketing now," says Ivan.

"The new model is affinity based on belief and behavior, not on a message but actually on what you do.

"And that is based, actually, on making people happy."

Summary

Trust requires mutuality – a belief that the other partner in the relationship has your best interest at heart. You can't broadcast trust and you can't build it behind closed doors. The pursuit of it shifts priorities. Profit becomes the KPI, not the objective.

G O A L　S T A T E / W O R S T　C A S E

Where does your business stand from 1 to 5?

Goal state (*scores 5/5*)

Stakeholders, partner-customers (members), employees have 100% trust in your organization's mission and motives as measured in 360-degree surveys. More than 90% of new business is generated by peer recommendation.

Worst case (*scores 1/5*)

Trust levels are measured at under 10%. More than 90% of new business is generated through marketing spend.

First **steps** …

If you estimate your organization scores poorly for trust:

1. The long answer: Become an Open Business. You can't build trust behind closed doors. Go back to Principle 1, and work your way through the rest.

2. The shorter answer: Start work on a relationship marketing strategy with the intent to create 10 Disney salt and pepper shaker stories a week.

3. What is your current investment in "creating goodwill"? Compare this to how highly you value trust. Adjust accordingly.

Summary

Open Business may be the future, but it is also, demonstrably, the present. The smartest organizations in the world are living by many of its principles.

Large heritage organizations such as Tesco, IBM, Fluor, Avis Budget Group, Grey London, and The Co-op are applying them to solve global problems or to reinvent themselves as fit for the 21st century.

The biggest success stories – Google, Amazon, Apple – are built on them.

Smaller, but rapidly growing businesses such as blur Group, giffgaff, Grow VC, Fairphone, Paperight, and NearDesk adopt them as first principles – the natural requirements of 21st-century business.

Whether you are running a giant PLC or planning your first start-up, there are advantages to be had from following the principles, lessons to be learned from those who have led the way.

Google CEO Eric Schmidt said: "In a networked world, trust is the most important currency." Make no mistake – you are living and working in a networked world.

The gift of Open is to bring stakeholders together in relationships of mutual trust.

Through shared beliefs (Purpose), shared risks (Open Capital), shared clients and objectives (Networked Organization), shared knowledge and collaborative activity (Shareability and Connectedness), shared ideas and rewards (Open Innovation), or shared intelligence and opportunities (Open

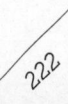

Data), the principles bring all stakeholders closer together to achieve shared aims: firms and employees, brands, customers, communities, financiers, and the world we all share.

Transparency gives us the governance and reassurance, being Member/Customer Led gives us the direction (to make our stakeholders our partners).

Trust is what the principles generate. Trust is what holds us together.

Trust is the most important currency in the networked world.

Open up and win.

Next steps ...

Table 1 The 10 Principles and your first steps for each

Principle	First Steps
1. Purpose: Clarify and communicate the "why" of your organization.	1. Ask key decision-makers and people who have been in the business a long time what they think the Purpose of the business is. If you get immediate consensus go to step 4. If not go to 2. 2. Investigate what is it about the organization that your members particularly believe in? What makes it different? Why did they choose it? 3. Sense-check a consensus shared belief against business needs. 4. List the things you do which align to your Purpose and the things that don't. 5. Stop doing the things that don't. Do more of the things that do.
2. Open Capital: Share the costs and risks and therefore the ownership and the passion through crowd-funding platforms or micro-capital investments.	1. Run an internal idea generation event at which users have play dollars to back their favorite ideas. 2. Test the winning idea on your preferred platform and commit to providing half the funding if the crowd will match the rest by pre-ordering the output. 3. Consider how you could offer equity in future projects to people outside of your business.

(continued)

Table 1 Continued

Principle	First Steps
3. Networked Organization: Focus on core competencies while enabling and supporting mutually beneficial activity inside and outside the organization.	1. Identify your core competencies. 2. Ask what – outside of these – are your staff doing? 3. Could you support those outside of your organization to achieve similar results? 4. Identify who can help you make that shift, and set time scales.
4. Shareability: Package knowledge for easy and open sharing internally and externally.	1. Discover how and why staff who already collaborate with their own tools and devices do so. 2. Consider what kind of Creative Commons licenses could work for you. 3. Recognize and reward staff for sharing what they know. 4. Identify and place a value on the business benefit you want to achieve through increased Shareability. 5. Allocate a budget based on the business benefit you seek to achieve. Resource for team flexibility. 6. Develop a plan informed by Connectedness.
5. Connectedness: Enable people within the organization to find what (or who) they need when they need it.	1. Set an example. Be visibly connected to the people and information you need to be through social media. 2. Conduct an audit of the collaboration tools and processes currently in use. 3. Decide on best practice for both to create a social platform for collaboration. 4. Deploy the platform as a replacement for, not an addition to, current activity.
6. Open Innovation: Bring customers and stakeholders into the innovation process to share the risk and reward of development.	1. Sponsor an internal hack day. 2. Learn from the process to see how you could shift to more open innovation processes, which could involve those from outside the organization. 3. Consider creating motivation through Purpose or reward.
7. Open Data: Make data available to those inside or outside of your organization who can make best use of it.	1. Identify the data you have available. 2. Assess which sets appear to have little value to you. 3. Make these available openly. 4. Consider corporate membership of the Open Data Institute.
8. Transparency: Make decisions openly, be honest about the criteria on which they are based.	1. Be proud of what you do. If you can't be proud of it, something is broken. Fix that first. 2. Ramp up the transparency by making people the boss of what they do. 3. Respond honestly to requests for information about the business.

(continued)

Table 1 Continued

Principle	First Steps
9. Member/Customer Led: Do things *with* your customers and staff rather than *to* them. Strive to treat them as genuine partners.	1. List how a partner should expect to be treated How does that map against how you regard your customers? 2. Test democracy with your staff. Report back on the opinions and the outcomes. 3. Build by defining areas for further democratic leadership by staff. Discover the limitations and think about what safeguards and controls will be appropriate.
10. Trust: Earn trust through your consistent actions over time.	1. The long answer: Become an Open Business. You can't build trust behind closed doors. Go back to Chapter 1, and start working. 2. The shorter answer: Start work on a relationship marketing strategy with the intent of creating 10 Disney salt and pepper shaker stories a week. 3. Review your current investment in "creating goodwill." Compare this to how highly you value trust. Adjust accordingly.

Continue the conversation, share your journey

Finally, to point out the obvious, this is a book. As such it forms a broadcast monologue, but it is also a conversation starter for the two-way flow of the network (the web).

This is the point at which the ideas contained within may continue to adapt through challenge and experience – your experience.

You will find a forum for those exploring Open Business at the Open Business Council Group on Linkedin.com. Just Google: "LinkedIn Open Business Council" and you'll be taken straight to it (or type www.linkedin.com/groups/Open-Business-Council-3973639 into your browser).

I will continue to publish updates on my learnings from working with some of the world's biggest businesses on my blog: FasterFuture.blogspot.com. If you would like to contact me directly, you'll find my email address there, too.

Alternatively, I encourage you to engage with me on Twitter, where I am @davidcushman. Use the hashtag #OpenBusiness to involve more people.

The greatest favor you can do me is to take the time to share your thoughts about this book in a review on Amazon – it is one of the most effective places to stimulate discussion about books and therefore inspire others to take the leap into the journey to Open Business.

I hope, by now, you will agree that it is a journey worth beginning.

Index